Stop-Motion Puppet Sculpting

Stop-Motion Puppet Sculpting

A Manual of Foam Injection, Build-Up, and Finishing Techniques

TOM BRIERTON

AUTHOR OF
Stop-Motion Armature Machining:
A Construction Manual (McFarland, 2002)

McFarland & Company, Inc., Publishers
Jefferson, North Carolina, and London

LIBRARY OF CONGRESS CATALOGUING-IN-PUBLICATION DATA

Brierton, Tom, 1957–
    Stop-motion puppet sculpting : a manual of foam injection,
build-up, and finishing techniques / Tom Brierton.
       p.   cm.
    Includes bibliographical references and index.

    ISBN 0-7864-1873-7 (softcover : 50# alkaline paper)

    1. Animation (Cinematography)   2. Puppet films.   3. Puppet
making.   4. Foam.   I. Title.
TR897.5.B7523   2004
791.43'34 — dc22   2004005501

British Library cataloguing data are available

Cover image: Djinn puppet, with underlying armature, sculpted by the
author

Manufactured in the United States of America

McFarland & Company, Inc., Publishers
  Box 611, Jefferson, North Carolina 28640
   www.mcfarlandpub.com

To the memory of John Emma

(September 16, 1951–January 30, 2003)

Fellow filmmaker, friend, puppet maker, and animator

Acknowledgments

I am indebted to Thomas R. Smith, who designed and sculpted the rat puppet detailed in the foam injection portion of this manual for my film *An Animated Audition*. Mr. Smith also took considerable time creating the **mold** and documenting the puppet's foam **running** and overall fabrication on video so that I could include the images in the manual. Many thanks, Tom! Thanks also to master mold-maker/foam runner Marie Cenkner and master animator Paul W. Jessel for sharing their thoughts on various aspects of **foam injection technique** over the years. Lastly, thanks to Ellen Marcus for her Minotaur conceptual designs.

And finally, to the Stopmotionanimation.com website, a huge Kraken-sized thank you for the wealth of information that all of you have contributed to the art form online. The site has become a stop-motion film college. Let's keep the classes going.

Tom Brierton
March 2004

Table of Contents

Preface

The following manual on **stop-motion** puppet fabrication, like its companion manual *Stop-Motion Armature Machining*, synthesizes the author's 30-plus years of puppet-making experience as it applies to the magical art form of stop-motion puppet animation. While there are a number of ways to build a stop-motion puppet, this book will focus on the two most common techniques:

1. Foam Injection

2. Build-up

Foam injection has been used primarily to create puppets for feature film productions. In America, many stop-motion practitioners used foam-injected puppets. Conversely, the early short subject puppet films tended to use the build-up technique to finish animation puppets. The "**Puppetoon**" shorts produced through Paramount Pictures by the Hungarian animator George Pal used the replacement animation technique. Pal and his associates built multiple models of a character, each posed in a slightly different manner than before, to convey motion. These replacement models were constructed from various materials, such as wood, glass, and metal.

The films of the great Russian puppet animator Ladislaw Starevitch used puppets that were generally "built up" from scratch, using many types of materials. Indeed, Starevitch seems to have used nearly every possible material to build his puppets, including cotton, glass, cloth, wood and balloons, to name just a few. In his short "The Mascot" (1934), Starevitch fitted a wire armature within a real chicken skeleton and animated it walking and running. Such applications might seem a bit morbid and bizarre, but the final effect is nonetheless quite engaging and startling.

This manual will outline the processes of foam injection and build-up techniques. Both techniques have their advantages and disadvantages. Both are very time-consuming. The final appearance of the puppet, whether fanciful, cartoonish, or lifelike, is determined not as much by the technique used, but by the skill and creative expertise of the sculptor/puppet maker. Many stop-motion puppets have been constructed that required little detail, while others have been sculpted so realistically that, in a photograph, the puppet is indistinguishable from a real animal or human. For example, to create a lifelike snake, the sculptor might acquire a real snakeskin, create a mold from that, and then pull **foam skin castings** from the mold. Since these foam skins were generated from a mold impression of actual snakeskin and are exact replicas of the real skin, the audience will perceive the illusion as real.

As readers proceed through the forthcoming chapters, they should keep in mind that the processes described herein are only a point of departure. They are a first step towards developing your own creative muse, in the course of building your own animation puppets. Take what you learn from these pages and further the art form by incorporating your own ideas and discoveries; if you stay with it, those discoveries are sure to follow. With this in mind, let's begin!

CHAPTER 1

Research, Design, Sketching and Sculpting

Inspiration for art comes to us in many ways and from many sources. We may be inspired by other art, a favorite piece of music, an historical event, a personal philosophy or world-belief system, a legend or myth, a deep personal loss, or our own imagination. Whatever the source, inspiration fuels the human creative endeavor. The 20th century French composer, Olivier Messiaen, was a devout Christian whose orchestral work, *La Transfiguration de Notre Seigneur Jesus-Christ*, and his more subdued four-movement *L'Ascension*, reflect his beliefs, namely, his desire to incorporate personal conviction into his works of art. Personal conviction born of one's belief system can be, and quite often is, a motivating factor for the creative works of our hands and minds. Whether we are creating a painting or composing a melody, penning a novel or drawing the elevation of a cruciform cathedral, creating movement on a dance floor or chiseling away at a marble sculpture, art is intensely personal. It is an extension of our beliefs, and the depth of our convictions.

Inspiration can be born unconsciously or consciously, and often comes when we least expect it, or when we aren't even looking for it. A worthwhile artistic idea can be born with very little thought — something triggers the left (creative) side of the brain and an idea is born. Or, we may wish to do something very specific (composing a fugue or painting a landscape), so we will sit at the piano or grab our canvas and brush and head off to an open glade. Conversely, a creative idea can often be extremely difficult to come up with when we are conscious of *wanting* to create a work of art. An artist discovers at some point in their life is that the creative idea usually comes when it is least expected.

Humans are deeply imitative creatures. We have a strong desire to re-create through the works of our hands objects that we see in life, and we have been doing just that for millennia. As far back as ancient Greece, the philosopher Aristotle thought of art as the reproduction of what is true (i.e. real) into something that is tangible (the works of our hands). For centuries humans have found great joy and pleasure in not only creating artistic visual representations of the world, but equally so, in viewing and touching them.

Research

Before beginning any design, it is imperative to take the time to research the subject that is to be designed and created. Students in college animation classes will often skip the research aspect and fly right into the design, and more often than not, their designs suffer, simply because they rely too much on memory. This can have disastrous results, for example, if a student is creating a fish, while never having been to an aquarium, let alone opened up a book on ichthyology.

The author built a dungeon set, pictured in Fig. 1-1, for his stop-motion animated short, "No Exit?" (1998). Months before set construction even began, many days were spent researching photographs, drawings, and engravings of dungeons. The author not only learned about the construction of dungeons and medieval prisons, but also many fascinating things about the architecture of the Middle Ages. Research is not a chore, but an education that is never wasted.

Figure 1-2

Figure 1-1

Figure 1-3

Large sheets of **foam core** were used to dress the walls. The cobblestone texture was simulated by using a small butane torch to melt the foam and create the space between the stones. The spaces were then painted with a dark color to help the cobblestones stand out (Fig. 1-2). It must be noted that foam core, when it is heated or burned, emits very toxic fumes. Any heating of foam core should be done with adequate ventilation or, preferably, outside, with a fire extinguisher on hand for any unforeseen accidents. Foam core is extremely flammable, so use common safety sense.

Items such as the rack, stockade, and ceiling column supports were manufactured from balsa wood (Fig. 1-3). The cobblestone-textured floor was created not with foam core, but rather spackling compound, which was then painted with the same paint used on the walls. In this instance, foam core would not have been effective, because foam is very soft,

and any attempt to **tie-down** the puppet with screws through the table would have crushed the foam. Hence, a much more solid substance was needed to withstand the pressure of the feet tie-downs.

Design and Sketching

After performing adequate research, the designing begins, generally with sketching. In fact, in musical composition, it is called just that: sketching. A composer spends countless hours, days, months or even years sketching a composition — writing themes, motifs, melodies, harmonic implications, considering the instrumental arrangement for the proposed work and more. Similarly, puppet design and sketching can be a gradual and evolving process. But the finished design can evoke feelings in the audience that go well beyond its visual impact, just as a piece of music can transport listeners to another time or place. The importance of design and sketching cannot be overstated, and they have much to do with how the finished work of art affects the observer.

Puppetry and Movement

BUILDING AND SCULPTING

With puppetry, we come to a curious convention when dealing with movement. On the one hand, puppets are, uniquely, sculptures. Like stone and marble sculpture, puppets can be enjoyed simply as works of art. But unlike sculpture for display, puppetry affords the added dimension of actual movement through space, as it applies to **real-time** marionette/rod puppets, or animation/time-lapse performance. They can therefore be thought of as a form of **kinetic sculpture**. An example of traditional kinetic sculpture would be a hanging mobile, or some other sculptural display in which the sculpture has real-time movement either thought mechanical, electrical, or human means.

Whether puppets are created for real-time stage performance or the animated film, the common amenity they share is expression through performance. Since this manual will concentrate specifically on stop-motion puppets, we can observe this phenomenon through the puppet's ability to be posed into virtually any form of expression. Observe Fig. 1-4.

This image is of a machined metal ball and socket armature for a stop-motion gorilla. Even without the covering of foam and hair to flesh out the puppet, by posing the armature in an ape-like gesture (in this case, one of defiance, surprise, and anger), we immediately understand what the character is feeling at that moment. To give the gesture an authentic feeling, the sculptor might observe gorillas in a documentary or at the zoo, to determine how they behave in a natural setting. In preparing for his stop-motion duties for the RKO film, *Mighty Joe Young* (1949), animator Ray Harryhausen spent time at the local zoo observing gorillas. He even went so

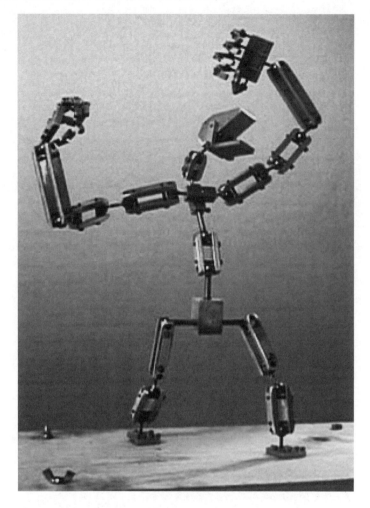

Figure 1-4

far as to become a vegetarian for a brief period in an attempt to live like a gorilla, so to speak. For the animation of the AT-AT walking machines in *The Empire Strikes Back* (1979), the animators spent time filming elephants so that they could get a sense of how a huge quadruped might walk.

Figure 1-5 illustrates the gorilla in a crouched position, walking forward. What is significant about this particular pose is *how* the gorilla is walking; that is, on its knuckles. Walking upright would not necessarily impart a simian gait. Dropping to his knuckles most certainly does. How will a puppeteer know this unless they observe a real gorilla in action? They won't, unless they take the time to do the research.

The Minotaur was a creature from Greek mythology that had the body of a human and the head of a bull. Figure 1-6 demonstrates the use of a **prototype** sculpture for a preliminary design for this character (as the reader will later see in Chapter 5,

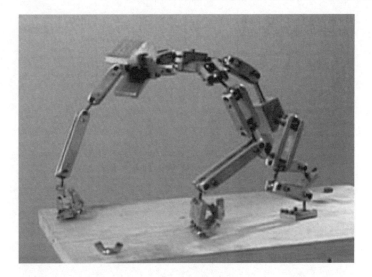

Figure 1-5

Figure 1-6

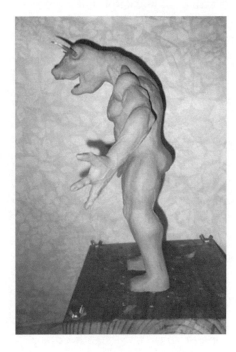

Figure 1-7

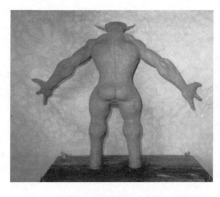

Figure 1-8

such a creature might possibly exist.

These prototype sculptures are sometimes referred to as maquettes, which are small detailed sculptures that serve as a three-dimensional sketch of a proposed concept.

this design will be further expanded on to create a final minotaur character). Viewing the model from different angles, we get a sense of the musculature making up the puppet (Fig. 1-7).

A fair amount of research was done to ensure anatomical accuracy, and to impart a natural feeling as when marrying the two seemingly unrelated elements (Fig. 1-8). It is not enough to simply join the anatomy of two different animals together; one must join them in a realistic manner, so that the viewer can sense that

A number of years ago, the author wished to create a stop-motion puppet of an elephant. Since he knew very little about the **physiology** of the elephant, he chose to spend time rendering a detailed color pencil drawing of two elephants in the wild (Fig. 1-9). Sketching and drawing is an excellent means of familiarizing oneself with the subject at hand. It also allows the artist to spend a good amount of time with the subject matter, in the process absorbing it into the memory and thoughts. The more you draw, the more you identify with and retain.

Figure 1-9

Later, the author began researching and designing a puppet for a djinn (Fig. 1-10), a mythological spirit from Middle Eastern folklore. The design itself was not too difficult; just the upper section of a human. No legs were necessary, because the puppet's performance only involved materializing from a lamp and hovering above it.

Figure 1-10

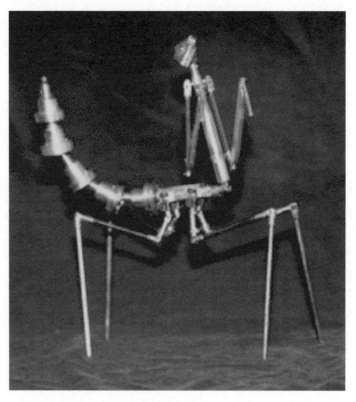

Figure 1-12

During the preliminary sculpting stage, a clay sculpture was created around the armature (Fig. 1-11). Often, the author will use sketches as a point of departure, using them only as references. Following them precisely can (though not always) stifle the creative process, which continues throughout the actual sculpting and creation of the puppet. This djinn model was initially drawn with a neutral mouth (plain, no specific expression). During the actual sculpting, it became apparent that this neutral mouth pose did not reflect the subtle menace of the djinn's character. This was remedied by imparting a slight smile onto the mouth, nothing overt, but just enough when coupled with the down-pointing brow to give the face an aura of ill will.

Figure 1-12 shows a metal armature that the author constructed for a praying mantis puppet. The design process included researching dozens of praying mantis photos; in the end a few were selected upon which to base the design of the puppet.

After the armature had been machined, it was then covered with foam that was built up over the metal (Fig. 1-13, 1-14). (Foam build-up technique will be discussed in Chapter Five.) To suggest the

Figure 1-11

Figure 1-13

Figure 1-14

smooth, wet-like chitinous surface of the **exoskeleton**, Vaseline was applied to the surface of the foam.

To recap, there is a basic approach to the development and sculpture the stop-motion puppet:

1. Research

2. Design (sketching/drawing the subject)

3. Building/sculpting the subject

By following this process, you will be well on your way to developing innovative and original art.

CHAPTER 2

The Sculpting Process

The Importance of Pose

The posing of all sculpture (narrative, abstract, or both) reveals a thought. In the case of an animation puppet (like all forms of animation: cel, computer, or stop-motion) that "thought" is found in the **key pose**. The performance animator's primary tool is the key pose, which tells the story or thought behind the character's behavior. Without an engaging key pose, a sculpture will be uninspired, shallow, and appropriately "thoughtless."

Key poses also rely a great deal on imaginary **arcs**, which are invisible lines that follow the form and contours of a shape. The arc principle is in fact the basis of all key-frame posing. Without it, we are left with very little as viewers to draw upon. Observe how in Figure 2-1, the crouching human figure has engaging movement in spite of the fact that it is sitting low to the ground and appears to be doing very little.

Conversely, notice that in Figure 2-2 the character seems to be in the same pose as Figure 2-1, but in fact, is not. The legs are straight across, the head looking down, and the arms down.

Figure 2-1

Arcs exist in Figure 2-2, but they are not specific to everyday human posture. As such, Figure 2-2 is a bland pose, and is not even remotely as interesting as Figure 2-1.

In Figure 2-1, the character's center of gravity is between the legs, while the torso is leaning over onto the left arm to keep him supported upright. The fact that the character is looking up at something also attracts the viewer's interest. Humans are, by nature, intensely curious creatures, and we desire to know who, what, when, where, and why. We see a story in Figure 2-1, and depending on how well the art engages us, we desire to know the *back-story* as well. *Who* is he? *What* is he doing? *When* is it taking place (during the Inquisition)? *Where* is he (in prison, and being forced to kneel)? *Why* is he looking up (is there a low-flying plane and he's ducking, or is he being forced to do something)? Once you have your viewers

Figure 2-2

asking questions, you have brought them into your character's world, and they will want to know more.

Sculpting Technique

There are two primary techniques used in sculpture: the **additive technique** and the **subtractive**. In the subtractive process, the sculptor removes material from the medium, for example a block of marble or piece of wood, to create the sculpture. The additive technique entails building up the sculpture by adding material. The most obvious additive material is clay. Clay has a unique advantage in that it can be either additive or subtractive, or a combination of the two. Clay is extremely versatile, and can also be pushed, pinched, melted, scraped, poked, and pulled.

The following discussion will explain the process of creating a wire armature for a clay sculpture, and the process of building the clay sculpture itself around the armature.

THE WIRE ARMATURE

There are a few schools of thought about creating a wire armature for a sculpture (throughout this manual, a wire armature will imply an armature for a stop-motion sculpture). Some people prefer making the wire armature in sections by making a wire piece for the arms, a wire section for the legs, and another section for the spine and neck-to-head assembly. The individual pieces are then assembled either by epoxying them together, or simply wrapping them together with smaller wire. In the following discussion, however, we will focus on creating the wire armature using a single piece of wire. The advantage of using a single wire piece is that it gives the armature extra strength. If separate pieces are assembled, there is a risk that the areas where they are joined will weaken over time.

Aluminum wire is a good choice for creating wire armatures, because it is relatively light, but is easy to bend and is sturdy. Wire with a ⅛-inch thickness will suffice.

Begin with a single roll of aluminum wire that you think is long enough to finish the form. Start by bending the wire into the form of the right foot (you can start with either foot, really, but for this illustration, we will begin with the right foot), as shown in Figure 2-3.

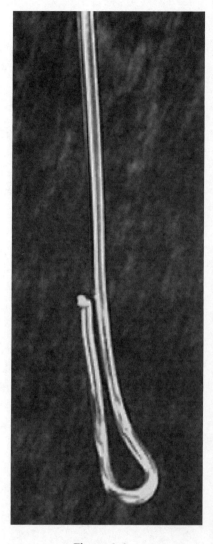

Figure 2-3

For reasons that will be explained later, leave a bit of wire extending up the shin of the leg, as illustrated.

Next, move upward to form the leg, then the pelvis and spine, and then over and down to create the right leg, spine, right shoulder and right arm (Fig. 2-4).

At this juncture, you will need to loop back up the arm and over to the center of the body to create the neck and head. Loop the wire so that you create a wrist that is parallel to the **ball and socket** of the hip joint. Now bend the wire so that you establish the neck, and then loop the wire so that it forms the head. Come back down the neck and bend it at the base of the neck, in the direction of the left arm (Fig. 2-5).

Now, bend the wire so that it forms the shape of the left arm (Fig. 2-6). Bend it back up so that it follows the arm, and then over to the spine. Follow the spine down to the pelvic area.

At this point, it is a good idea to secure the wire formation with smaller-gauge wire. The wire armature

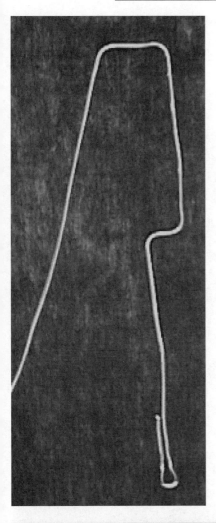

Figure 2-4

is probably starting to flop about a bit, which makes it difficult to maintain proper proportions for the figure. Take a roll of smaller gauge wire (1/16 inch will suffice, and it can either be mild steel, copper, brass, or aluminum), and begin wrapping the armature with it (Fig. 2-7).

Wrapping the figure with the smaller gauge wire draws the double looped wire tightly together. Proceed to wrap the smaller wire up the arm, up the neck, and down the other arm.

Once the upper portion is secured with the smaller gauge wire, continue looping the larger gauge wire to finish the armature. Form the left leg and then come back up over the leg, and into the center of the pelvis (Fig. 2-

8). If you need to reinforce the sturdiness of the leg, wrap it with the smaller gauge wire.

Finally, come back down the right leg, and cut the wire so that it overlaps the piece of wire that you began with (Fig. 2-9).

Now we see the purpose of extending the wire of the right foot halfway up the shin. Because the two wires are overlapping, the right ankle is stronger after it is wrapped with the smaller gauge

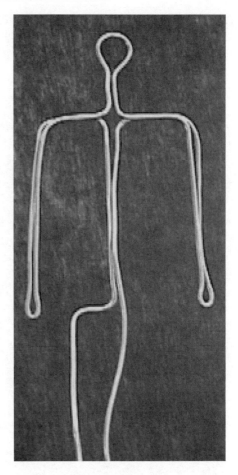

Figure 2-6

Figure 2-5

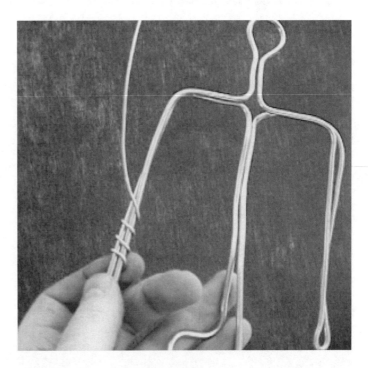

Figure 2-7

wire. Continue wrapping the rest of the armature with the smaller wire until you are finished (Fig. 2-10).

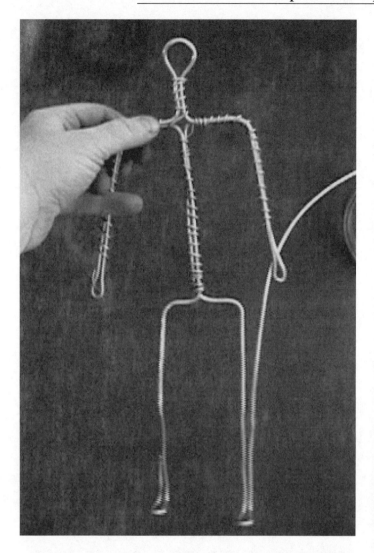

Figure 2-8

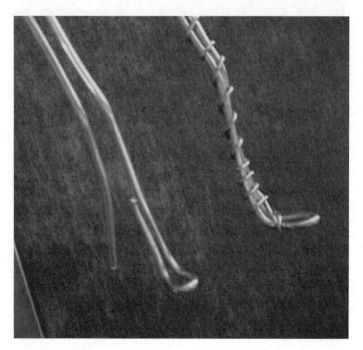

Figure 2-9

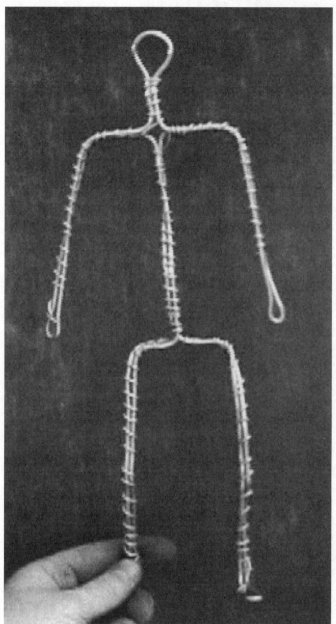

Figure 2-10

Now that the wire armature is complete, we can proceed to the next step: anchoring it to a sculpting table. The author prefers to use a modification of the **potter's wheel** to hold the armature in place while sculpting (Fig. 2-11).

Figure 2-11

This is a homemade turntable, and has a **lazy Susan** between the bottom two boards. The lazy Susan allows the table to turn 360 degrees, enabling the sculptor to easily view the sculpture at all angles while working.

The next step is to pinch the feet with pliers so that they can accommodate the screws used to anchor the armature to the table (Fig. 2-12).

Figure 2-12

The wire armature can now be mounted on the work table (Fig. 2-13).

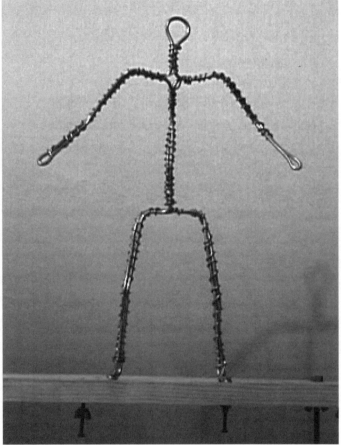

Figure 2-13

BLOCKING OUT THE FIGURE

Once the armature is prepared and mounted, the task of sculpting the character can begin, in this case by first blocking out the basic shapes and contours of the muscles. At this stage, it isn't necessary to add minute detail. The first step is to block everything out. Smoothing and finessing the piece will come later.

In this example, we will sculpt a dancing woman step-by-step from clay, using the additive technique. The sculpture will be roughed out, rather than finely detailed. Especially when working with the human form, roughing in the contours, muscles, and bones of the body can be an important part of the creative process, revealing fascinating insights as the sculptor proceeds.

Figure 2-14 provides us with an illustration of the proposed sculpture. As you begin to sculpt, it is sometimes a good idea to block the muscles out directly over the armature. This allows you get a feel for how the sculpture is progressing, and how it looks anatomically. Smoothing and detailing the surface comes later.

Figure 2-15

Figure 2-14

We will not be going for detailed anatomical realism, but for a more stylized look. The torso is turned to the front to prepare the dancer for her next move, and her right foot is up on the ball of her foot as if to anticipate that move. Her long flowing hair dangles backward from her head as it tilts back. Bend the wire armature into the shape of the sketch (Fig. 2-15).

From a side view, the armature's center of gravity, within the hips, must be moved to the center of the body, between the feet(Fig. 2-16). If this is not done, the gravitational centerline will appear abnormal.

Now that the armature is posed, we can begin applying lumps of clay, blocking out the muscles and contours as we go along. It does not matter where you begin applying the clay, though the author

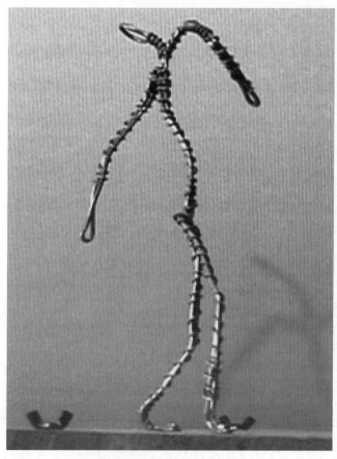

Figure 2-16

prefers starting at the hips. A number of different clays (both oil-based and water-based) are available on the market. One clay that works very well (and that can even be melted down and poured into molds) is **Van Aiken** clay. This oil-based clay is a good material to use for life masks and stop-motion puppet sculptures.

The hips (pelvis) of a woman are wider than the hips of a man (to accommodate childbirth), and the clay is placed in such a way as to create the proper effect (Fig. 2-17).

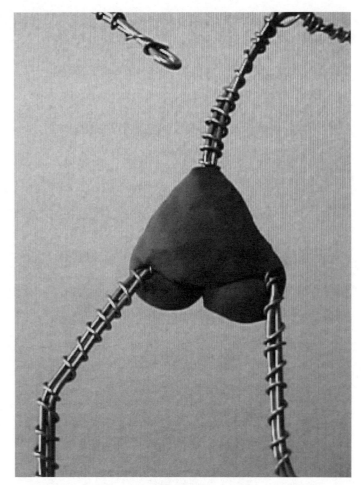

Figure 2-18

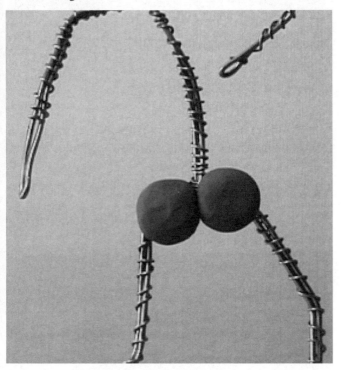

Figure 2-17

The next step is to form the stomach area over the front of the abdomen (Fig. 2-18). In additive sculpture, one might think of layering the muscles over one another. In the following sculpture, only the major muscles and primary bones are sculpted into the form.

Notice that in Fig. 2-19, the leg, calf, thigh and part of the hip are formed. The calf muscle is clearly distinct. The kneecap is visible as well; it was formed simply by pinching the clay which results in a set of indentations on either side of the knee area.

Note, too, that the realistic appearance of the knee is enhanced by the shape of the patella bone be-

neath the skin, rather than by the shape of a specific muscle. In short, there are two amenities of an organic body that account for its form: muscle shapes, and bone structures that lay beneath the skin and muscle.

Figure 2-19

Clay is added to the spine to beef up the torso area (Fig. 2-20). As the clay is added, shape it to conform to the ribcage. Since a woman's waist is generally thinner between the top of the hips and the bottom of the ribcage, that area can be pinched in, which in turn accentuates the girth of the hips. Conversely, the sides of the waist of a male are generally much flatter. Notice, too, that in Fig. 2-20, we see the form of the pelvic bone beginning to take shape (just above the hip).

Figure 2-20

In Fig. 2-21 we pinch the sides of the shin muscles, which helps to form the curvature of the calf muscle. One of the best models to reference while sculpting is your own body. Observe in a mirror how your own muscles flex, how they behave when they move. Note too the shape of the bones beneath your skin. Observing these forms in real life will aid you greatly in developing a sense, through practice, of proper placement of bones and muscles on an organic body. Artists with the financial resources might hire a professional model to pose while they sculpt or draw life studies. Learning from real life, obviously,

is the best way to acquire the skills needed to become a successful sculptor.

Figure 2-21

Notice in Fig. 2-22 that the torso is leaning to the left, causing the left side of the ribs to bulge outward. Conversely, the ribs on the right side of the body are much straighter. As the torso leans to the left, the skin on the right side becomes taut over the ribs.

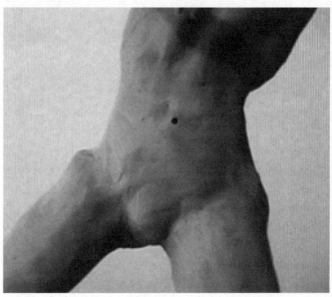

Figure 2-22

Viewing the sculpture from the back, we must create the illusion that the skin is being pinched on the left side of the lower ribs as the torso lists toward the left. This is because the lower rib bones force the skin down at the crease, thus creating a few wrinkles in the skin. In Fig. 2-23, a flat pointed spade-like tool is used to cut small creases into the clay, thus creating the necessary wrinkles in the skin. The glutei muscles of the buttocks are also further smoothed out and rounded.

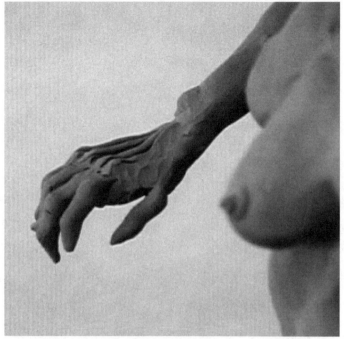

Figure 2-24

bottom to form the knuckle and bone joints (Fig. 2-25).

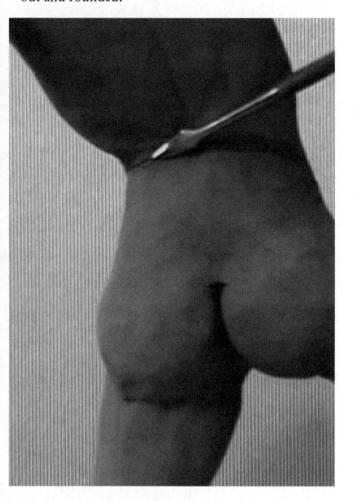

Figure 2-23

Hands are especially challenging to sculpt because of their delicate curves and features. Observe your own hand as you sculpt. Notice how the first and third fingers are approximately the same length, while the middle finger is the longest, and the fourth finger the shortest. The thumb begins at the base of the palm, and comes up halfway the length of the first finger (Fig. 2-24). Each finger has three representative bone joints: the knuckle where the finger joins with the palm, the middle joint, and the third toward the top of the finger. The prominent wrist bone is also brought out.

Each finger can be rolled from a piece of clay, cut to length, and pinched at the top, middle and

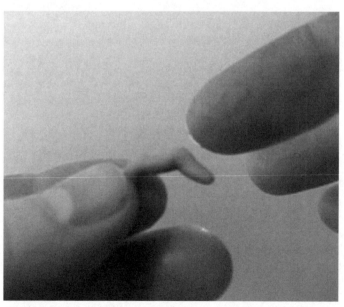

Figure 2-25

The fingers are then attached to the front of the palm and the joins smoothed out.

The upper torso is now fleshed out more, pinching and pulling the muscles of the arms, neck, head, and abdomen (Fig. 2-26). Here again, the best way to duplicate these forms is to observe how your own arms flex. If one is available, set up a large mirror and use yourself as a model, flexing and moving your arms, neck, and torso about so that you can see what is happening with your bones and muscles. In the case of Fig. 2-26, the abdominal muscles were created by taking two pieces of clay and pushing them together side-by-side onto the stomach area. They were then smoothed out with the fingers into the outer portion of the ribcage. In this way, a natural crease was formed between the abdominal muscles, just as occurs on a real body.

around the nipples) and the nipples should be positioned correctly if one is to accurately describe the breasts' form. These are placed at the center, toward the lower half of the breasts.

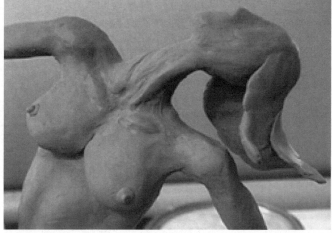

Figure 2-27

Figure 2-26

In Fig. 2-27, the upper portion of the torso has been blocked out. Two round pieces of clay were formed and placed onto the chest to represent the breasts. Since the breasts of a female protrude from the chest and hang loosely, it is necessary to consider how they react to the position of the torso in relation to gravitational pull. Since the figure's torso is leaning to the left, the left breast is sculpted to hang more loosely than the right breast. Certainly, gravity is pulling both breasts, but the left one is affected more by this leaning-to-the-left action. The upward position of the right arm brings the right breast up somewhat so that it does not fall down as much as the left one. Finally, the areolas (the rings of skin

To create a realistic impression of the head falling back on the neck, the sternomastoid muscles are accentuated. These are the two muscles on both sides of the front of the neck that allow flexing of the head (Fig. 2-27). The raised objects just above the breasts and between the shoulders are the clavicle bones.

The sculpture is turned to the side in Fig. 2-28, and then to the front in Fig. 2-29. It is a good practice to periodically turn the sculpture as one is working, observing the progress from all angles. This helps to keep the "three-dimensionality" of the work on track. The danger of working from only one view is that the

Figure 2-28

sculpture may look fine from that particular perspective, but the moment it is turned, glaring mistakes can become apparent, including lopsidedness, disproportionate volume (i.e. inconsistencies of muscle mass from leg to leg, or from arm to arm), and asymmetrical muscularity.

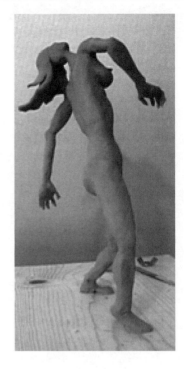

Figure 2-31

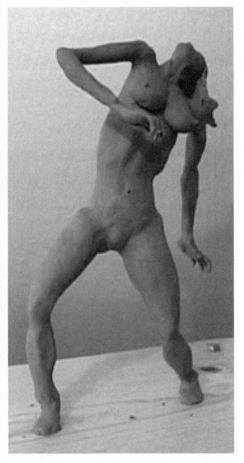

Figure 2-29

As you turn the sculpture while working, shape the muscles with your fingers, pushing and moving them into place until a sense of naturalness is achieved (Fig. 2-34). This realistic appearance, more often than not, is a result of working the clay into shape, then walking away from the work for a brief

Figure 2-30

time, then returning to the sculpture with a fresh eye and examining any possible abnormalities.

By turning the sculpture once again (Fig. 2-30), we can examine the proportions from still another view.

Once the sculpture has been blocked out and formed to some degree, you can experiment with the dynamics of the form by placing the viewer in a low angle (Fig. 2-31). From this angle, the sculpture is more interesting than when viewed from the side or the front, and the sense of movement is apparent.

CHAPTER 3

The Foam Injection Technique

Making the Mold

Of the two most common types of foam puppet making (**foam injection** and **build-up**), foam injection is the more common. The foam injection process is a technique for forming foam rubber around an existing puppet armature. Foam injection itself has been practiced for many decades, and the process has remained relatively unchanged. The only significant change has been the development of better foam products and foam mixing techniques. The theory of foam injection is relatively simple, while the actual hands-on process takes some acquired skill and patience. The images presented in this chapter are of a comical, "cartoony" rat character, and we will follow the character's development through the various steps of the foam injection construction process.

The foam injection process can be outlined in eight steps:

1. Preparation (wrapping) of the armature
2. Sculpting the clay prototype sculpture
3. Creating the mold
4. Mixing the foam
5. Injecting the foam into the **mold cavity**
6. Curing the mold in a **convection oven**
7. Removing the foam casting from the mold
8. Detailing and painting the casting

PREPARING THE ARMATURE

Each step has its own set of challenges, which must be mastered through practice. The armature, regardless of the material from which it is constructed, must be protected from the clay that will be sculpted around it. This is particularly true for machined metal joints (Fig. 3-1), where clay can push into and fill areas of the joints and can (though not always) gum up the joint itself. This really isn't a major problem. The real struggle comes after the mold is finished and the clay sculpture removed from the mold

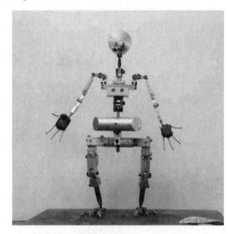

Figure 3-1

cavity. The clay must be removed from the armature, and if there is residual clay inside the joints, the armature will need to be taken apart and each part cleaned. This can take up valuable production time. To prevent this, it is generally best to wrap the armature before sculpting the character in clay (Fig. 3-2).

If your character has a lot of surface area (such as a heavyset character, like Santa Claus), the sculpting process will require a lot of clay. This can make the sculpture rather heavy and difficult to handle.

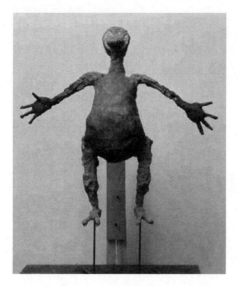

Figure 3-2

One way to reduce the amount of clay used and to save money, as well as sculpting and production time, is to bulk the armature up with wrapping material. There are different kinds of wrapping material. Aluminum foil and plastic wrap are good choices. Aluminum foil in particular is well suited for this step, because it holds its shape when crinkled, and can easily be wrapped around the surface of the armature.

Sculpting the Prototype

SECURING THE ARMATURE

Notice that in Fig. 3-3, a **pylon dowel rod** going

Figure 3-3

into its back is suspending the armature. Additionally, there are two long screws going into the tie-down holes of the feet. This serves a twofold purpose: the sculpture is stabilized so that it is less likely to wobble or fall over dur-

ing the sculpting process, and it allows for space underneath the sculpture when it is laid down horizontally for the inclusion of the clay wall, which will separate the two mold halves.

To accommodate the pylon screw support going into the back of the sculpture, a hole must be drilled beforehand into the piece of the armature that forms the pelvic area, and tapped the same size thread as the rod support.

The Prototype in Clay

USING HAIR FOR THE SURFACE

When doing the initial sculpture in clay, is it best to smooth the skin first. Detail (such as hair, wrinkles, warts, scales, etc.) can be added afterwards. In the case of this rat, the sculptor opted to smooth the surface of the rat first (Fig. 3-4, 3-5). Initially, the idea was to use an actual hair felt. It has been a common practice for decades to cover stop-motion puppets with actual hair. The choice of the hair used is determined to some extent by the scale of the completed puppet. For example, if a client needs a stop-motion puppet of a mouse, a mouse armature could be fabricated that is the size of a real mouse (three inches, approximately, excluding tail length)—an easily manageable scale for animation. If the puppet were built so that it was the size of a real mouse, then it would be appropriate to use a real mouse hide to cover the armatured puppet, since the fur of a real mouse would fit the scale of the puppet mouse. Most stop-motion puppets, though, are built between eight to 18 inches tall, and the proper fur must be used to match the scale.

In the case of the giant ape, King Kong (*King Kong*, 1933, RKO Productions), the puppet was approximately 14 to 15 inches tall. The modelers used rabbit fur for the puppet's hair; since the average length of a rabbit is roughly 14 to 15 inches, rabbit fur was of the proper scale to look proportional on a puppet of approximately the same size. The general rule of thumb is to use hair that comes from an animal that is roughly the size of the puppet itself.

A History of Rubberizing Animal Fur

The process of rubberizing animal fur by hand has become somewhat antiquated, due to the availability of synthetic stretchable furs. Still, a process developed by an MGM staff **taxidermist** was quite ingenious, and deserves discussion here.

During the production of *Mighty Joe Young* (RKO,1949), visual effects supervisor Willis H. O'Brien contacted taxidermist George Lofgren. O'Brien wanted to use Lofgren's patented technique for rubberizing animal hides to make the ape puppet's fur covering. In theory, the process is relatively simple. Lofgren would select the hide of a recently killed animal. The hair was combed out so that it would lie flat and smooth, and then a washable adhesive was painted over the hair.

After the adhesive dried, Lofgren would lay the hide into a container with a sealable lid, with the skin facing up. This container also housed the larvae of a species of *Dermestes* beetle. The larva of the *Dermestes* will eat anything organic, save for non-digestible items like hair and fingernails. Once the skin was eaten away, the hide was removed. Since the larvae had not eaten the hair, the bottom follicles of the hair stems were now exposed. And the hair, because it was still joined together via the adhesive, would not fall apart. Lofgren then took the hide and brushed the follicle side with a few coats of rubber latex. After the latex dried, he flipped the hide over and washed the adhesive from the hair. Since the hair follicles were now embedded into the latex rubber, the hair would not fall out, and the hide could then be wrapped around an animation puppet or taxidermied animal.

Sculpting the Surface in Clay

In the case of the rat sculpture pictured, the hair texture was sculpted directly into the clay, rather than using a fur pelt. Since the character was intended to look "cartoony" and not realistic, a fur pelt for the puppet was not deemed necessary. This decision also saved a bit of production time as well. It was faster to sculpt hair texture into the clay than it

Figure 3-4

would have been to acquire a stretchable fur pelt, then fit it around the model.

In Figures 3-4 and 3-5, the sculpture has been blocked out and smoothed. The next step is to begin sculpting the hair texture itself.

It was decided that the hair should lie flat on the surface of the sculpture (Fig. 3-6), so that it would appear smoothed and combed during performance animation.

Figure 3-5

Figure 3-6

To create softer textures with sharp pointed tools (and to keep residual clay from building up on the tip of a sculpting tool), you can sometimes place a barrier between the tool and the clay. In Fig. 3-7, a piece of light, clear plastic is laid on the surface of the clay. Pressing into the plastic with the sculpting tool creates an indentation in the clay. The plastic can then be moved to another section of the sculpture and used to create more textures.

Figure 3-8

Figure 3-7

Figures 3-8, 3-9 and 3-10 reveal the finished textured clay sculpture. The hands, belly, and snout were left smooth to suggest fleshy skin.

Figure 3-9

Figure 3-10

Building the Mold

PREPARING THE WORK AREA

Like most mold-making processes, you should work on a clean flat surface with ample room. The amount of room needed is dictated by the dimensions of the final mold, which can be calculated by measuring the dimensions of the clay sculpture. In the case of our rat friend, we find his dimensions to be 15 inches tall, 9 inches wide, and 4 inches deep (the tail will be cast separately, and joined to the body via a square brass post). With this information, we now know that our worktable area must at least exceed those dimensions. Fig. 3-11 illustrates an appropriate area for making the mold.

Figure 3-11

Mold-making materials are rather messy, so it is a good idea to cover your work area with heavy-duty paper, such as construction paper, or generous layers of newspaper (Fig. 3-12).

Figure 3-12

To prevent the paper from sliding around, heavy-duty tape (masking, duct, etc.) can be used to stabilize the paper onto the working surface (Fig. 3-13).

Figure 3-13

SECURING THE MODEL

The clay sculpture must now be mounted to a surface of some kind, in order to brace and support the sculpture during the formation of the first half of the mold. Since you will want to turn the model around while you are mounting it to its base, it is often practical to place the brace onto a **lazy Susan** (Fig. 3-14). The lazy Susan is a rotating device that works on a series of ball bearings. They can be purchased from a hardware store, and are almost always pre-assembled. Either screws or rivets hold two plates together, and between these two plates is a groove with ball bearings. The plates can then be rotated independently. A mounting board can be fixed onto the bottom plate, and another board affixed to the top plate. In this way, the top board can be rotated 360 degrees.

Figure 3-14

The finished clay sculpture is now brought over to the lazy Susan and placed on the top rotating board (Fig. 3-15).

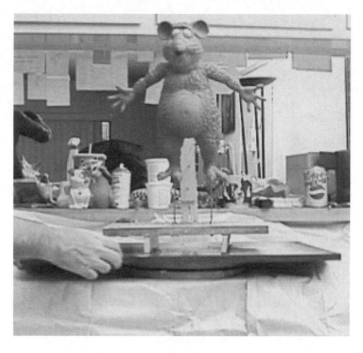

Figure 3-15

Rotate the sculpture a few times and inspect it a final time for any imperfections or damage that might have resulted from moving it about. If all is well and you are ready to begin creating the first clay wall, lay the puppet down on the lazy Susan (Fig. 3-15), so that its front is facing up (this will allow us to pour the front half of the mold). The pylon that is attached to its rear should support its back.

Figure 3-16

With the clay sculpture now suspended and supported, two blocks of wood are placed underneath the sculpture at the feet, and one above the head. A board (such as a piece of foam core board) can now

Figure 3-17

be placed on top of the boards and underneath the sculpture (Fig. 3-17).

THE CLAY SEPARATION WALL

With this board in place, you can now begin forming the clay wall around the circumference of the sculpture. This step is somewhat laborious, in that you have to very carefully bring the clay up to the edge of the sculpture, *ALL* the way around it. Since this particular sculpture will only need two halves to form its mold (a half for the front, and a half for the back) this clay wall separation only needs to come up halfway on the sculpture. Continue forming the clay wall until you have completely covered the bottom of the sculpture, and have made certain that there are no gaps between it and the clay wall (Fig. 3-18). If there are gaps, then the mold-making material (in this case, we will be using Ultra-cal-30) will seep beneath the sculpture when you

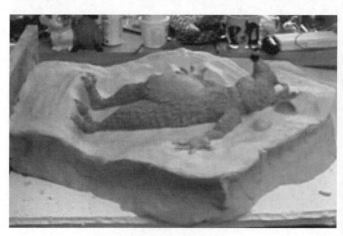

Figure 3-18

pour it on, covering portions of the backside of the sculpture and preventing you from making the second half of the mold.

In Fig. 3-18, the sculpture is now imbedded into the clay wall slab. Note the **registration keys** (the

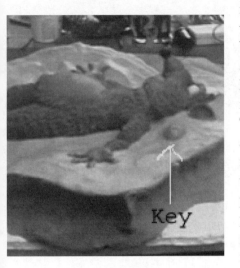

Figure 3-19

round shapes), which should be placed at the sides of the head and at the feet (Fig. 3-19). This will ensure a proper fit when the two dried mold pieces are placed back together for the foam injection process.

Figure 3-20

PREPARING THE SURFACE

Once the mold separation is finished, you need to prepare the surface of the clay (both the mold separation as well as the front of the clay sculpture) so that it can be easily removed from the Ultracal, after the Ultracal has dried. One product that works very well for this purpose is Crystal Clear Krylon spray, which can be purchased at almost any art supply house. This is a glossy, clear plastic acrylic in an aerosol can. It puts a plastic coating on the clay to prevent it from sticking to other surfaces (in this case, the other half of the mold).

Begin by spraying a coat or two of acrylic onto the surface of the clay separator and the front of the sculpture (Fig. 3-20). Once this is applied, cover the surface with dulling spray or talcum powder to make it less tacky.

MIXING THE MOLD MATERIAL

With the clay separation wall now treated with the separators, the next step is to mix up the mold-

making material. There are a number of stone-based materials that can be used to make the mold. **Plaster** is another option, but plaster chips or breaks easily if not handled carefully. One product that is often used for making mask and puppet molds is **Ultracal-30** (Fig. 3-21). Other products puppetmakers use include are hydrostone and hydrocal. Ultracal is denser than plaster and is really more similar to concrete, and it captures the surface detail of a clay sculpture very well. It can, however, get quite heavy as the mold gets larger.

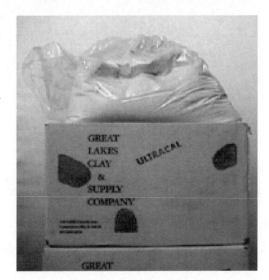

Figure 3-21

Ultracal comes as a grayish powder that must be mixed with water. To begin mixing, you will need a large plastic bowl and a container to hold water (Fig. 3-22).

Pour water into the bowl and add the Ultracal little by little, mixing as you go. Working time for Ultracal is determined by the thickness of the mix. The thinner it is, the longer it takes to set. While a

Figure 3-22

Figure 3-24

large wooden spoon is good for mixing Ultracal, the best way to ensure that all of the lumps and air pockets have been removed from the mixture is to mix it with your hands (Fig. 3-23). It is messy, so mix near a sink and have clean-up materials on hand.

Often, a small brush will work well to drip and smooth the Ultracal over the sculpture's surface (Fig. 3-25). Be careful not to brush too hard, or you can easily destroy the surface texture of the sculpture that you have laboriously worked on for days or weeks.

Figure 3-23

Figure 3-25

Pouring the Mold

Since we will be pouring the pitcher of Ultracal directly onto the surface of the sculpture and clay wall, the mixture should be fairly liquid, but not too thin. This comes only with practice. You want it thin enough so that it will pour over the surface of the sculpture fairly easily, but it must also be thick enough so that when it is poured, it will not flow over the sides of the clay separation. Gently cover the surface of the sculpture with the mixed Ultracal (Fig. 3-24).

Keep adding the Ultracal until the sculpture is almost completely covered (Fig. 3-26). Note, too, that in Fig. 3-26, a clay wall has been built up beneath the feet. This particular mold is actually going to be comprised of three pieces; one for the back, the front, and the bottom of the feet. Since the bottoms of the feet are going to be cast as well, they need to be isolated within their own mold cavity. Remember, too, that the feet have two screws coming from their tie-down holes (Fig. 3-15), which are in turn anchored into the wooden support. Once the mold for the bottom of the feet has been made, these screws can be extracted with pliers.

Figure 3-26

Make certain that every part of the sculpture is covered and that nothing is exposed (Fig. 3-27).

Figure 3-27

Continue layering the Ultracal over the sculpture until you have built up a mound that covers it entirely (Fig. 3-28). Let the Ultracal set overnight.

The following day, the Ultracal should be cool to the touch, indicating that it has completely set up. You can now turn the entire configuration over on its side and strip off the clay separator (Fig. 3-29a, 3-29b). This exposes the back of the sculpture. Be extremely careful when doing this, because accidentally dropping the mold or brushing up against the back of the sculpture can ruin the detail.

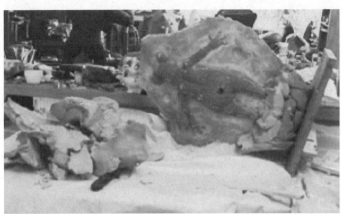

Figure 3-29a

Figure 3-29b

The next step is to paint the surface of the Ultracal and the sculpture surface with a **release agent**. Ultracal adheres to itself, but this agent will prevent the solidified mold half from fusing with the other half of the mold when it is poured. Vaseline petroleum jelly is a very simple and inexpensive release agent that works very well (Fig. 3-30).

Figure 3-28

Figure 3-30

Using a small paint brush, brush a layer of Vaseline onto the surface of the mold. You can be somewhat liberal in layering the Vaseline, but put on just enough to give the surface a smooth, slick surface (Fig. 3-31).

Figure 3-31

Vaseline can also be applied to the surface of the sculpture with a brush, but it must be done very carefully to avoid damaging or destroying the surface texture of the sculpture (Fig. 3-32).

In the example of the rat sculpture, it is important to remember that the hair texture is sculpted onto the surface. Applying too much Vaseline to the surface will invariably fill in the textured markings, and the Ultracal will not pick up this detail when you pour the second half of the mold.

Mix another batch of Ultracal into a loose pasty consistency, and pour onto the back of the sculpture, covering it completely.

Figure 3-32

To ensure that both halves of the mold can be separated easily, you must create a series of clay **prying keys** that go around the perimeter of the mold (Fig. 3-33).

Figure 3-33

These keys should be shaped into squares (Fig. 3-34). Once the other half of the mold is poured and the halves separated, the clay keys will be removed to expose open areas where a prying tool can be inserted.

Figure 3-34

Fig. 3-35 demonstrates the proper placement of prying keys around the edge of the mold half.

Figure 3-35

REINFORCING THE MOLD

Once the back of the clay sculpture is covered with the first layer of Ultracal, this half of the mold will be finished by layering it with reinforcing strips of **hemp** cloth (Fig. 3-36).

Figure 3-36

Hemp is a fiber that absorbs nearly anything water-based (in this case, Ultracal). Saturating hemp cloth strips with Ultracal and applying them will strengthen the mold significantly. Should the mold crack or break after it is dried, the hemp will keep the pieces together until the damage can be repaired.

After the initial layer has been poured over the sculpture (see Fig. 3-35), prepare to begin layering the hemp strips. Cut the hemp cloth into strips, and mix up a batch of Ultracal. This batch needs to be thinner than what was poured over the sculpture; the

consistency should be smooth and free-flowing, and less like a paste.

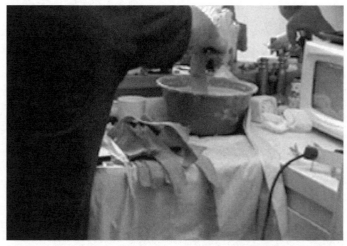

Figure 3-37

Dip a strip of hemp into the Ultracal (Fig. 3-37) and lay it over the sculpture (Fig. 3-38).

Figure 3-38

Continue doing this until you have completely covered the sculpture and have built up a small mound (Fig. 3-39).

Next, smooth the surface of the mound by wetting the palm of your hand and gently rubbing it over the surface of the wet Ultracal (Fig. 3-40).

This results in a very smooth top surface that is not rough to the touch when dried, and that also looks aesthetically pleasing (Fig. 3-41). As before, let this half of the Ultracal mold set overnight.

Figure 3-39

Figure 3-40

Figure 3-41

After the mold has dried, remove the wing nuts from the screws that are holding the feet onto the board, and remove the board itself.

The next step is to remove the Ultracal foot support from the bottom (Fig. 3-42, 3-43). When doing this, be careful not to accidentally bend the screws going into the bottoms of the feet.

Figure 3-42

Figure 3-43

Figure 3-44 shows the space where the Ultracal foot support was. The wing nuts have been placed back on the screws.

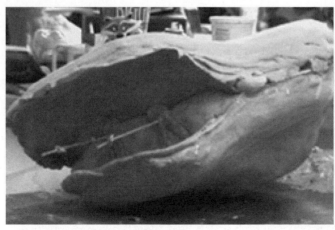

Figure 3-44

Separating the Mold Halves

Separating the mold halves from each other is somewhat tricky, and takes a lot of patience. Do not try to separate them quickly, or they may crack.

Begin by removing the clay keys with a small screwdriver or similar tool (Fig. 3-45).

Figure 3-45

Once the clay keys are removed, take a screwdriver and a rubber mallet, and very gingerly go around each key area, gently tapping the screwdriver into the hole (Fig. 3-46).

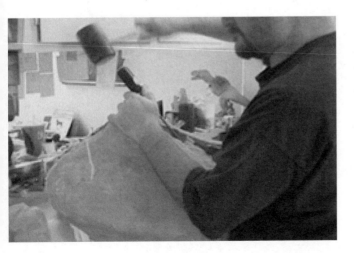

Figure 3-46

Eventually, a small crack will begin to form around the perimeter, where the two halves meet, and as you continue tapping, this crack will become

more pronounced. When it grows wide enough to grab with your fingers, stand the mold on its end, and slowly pull the two halves apart (Fig. 3-47). The clay sculpture may or may not come out intact, depending on whether enough Vaseline was used to separate it effectively. Whether or not it comes out intact is inconsequential, because the mold is fabricated, and the clay sculpture has served its purpose. The clay can now be stripped from the armature, and the mold cavities must be cleaned of residual clay.

Figure 3-47

Creating Foam Bleed-Off Conduits

The final step in the mold construction process is to take a sharp, fine-pointed tool (such as a dentist's scraper), and scrape small foam conduits extending from the edges of the fingers, toes, ears, body and head to the outer edge of one of the mold pieces (either piece is fine). When the foam is injected into the mold cavity (which will be explained in the next chapter), these conduits will allow excess foam to bleed off after the cavity has been filled (Fig. 3-48).

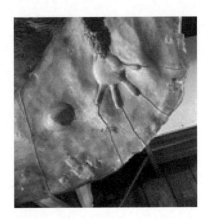

Figure 3-48

CHAPTER 4

Mixing and Injecting Hot Foam Latex

To master foam mixing (or **foam running**, as it is called in professional circles) requires a lot of patience and practice. Two types of foam are used to create stop-motion puppets: hot foam and cold foam. Throughout the following procedure, we will be working only with hot foam. Hot foam is so named because it must be cured in a **convection oven** to properly set (there is one exception to this, which will be discussed in the next chapter).

A number of suppliers manufacture hot foam, and all brands have mixing requirements specific to the maker. In fact, even with individual brands, the consistency of the foam can vary from batch to batch. Because of this, it is generally not a good practice to mix different batches of foam when making a puppet. We will be using GM Foam, which is named for Gil Mosko, the foam's inventor and supplier. Mr. Mosko manufactures and sells his brand of hot foam in Van Nuys, California. A list of suppliers that sell GM Foam is provided in the back of this manual.

GM Foam comes in four parts:

1. Liquid latex

2. Foaming agent

3. Curing agent

4. Gelling agent

Also included in the kit is a jar of mold release agent.

The latex is pure latex and must be mixed with the other ingredients before it can expand and set. Most, if not all, hot foams have an ammonia base that must evaporate during the mixing process before the foam can set properly. Because of this, the foam has a strong pungent odor, and so adequate ventilation is necessary, as well as a breathing respirator coded for ammonia. Continual inhalation of ammonia fumes can cause one's blood pressure to rise, and this is particularly important for people with hypertension to remember.

Preparing the Mold for Foam Injection

Once the mold parts have been cleaned of residual clay, the next step is to treat each mold half with a mold release agent (Fig. 4-1). The release agent will help prevent the foam from sticking to the mold walls as you are pulling the foam casting out after it has been cured in an oven and allowed to cool. Release agents vary from supplier to supplier, and one is generally included with the foam kit.

To prepare the mold with release agent, take one half of the mold and begin gently brushing the release agent into the impression cavity of the mold half (Fig. 4-2). A small paintbrush will suffice.

Figure 4-1

Figure 4-2

As you are brushing, be careful not to coat the mold cavity too heavily. This is particularly important if the original surface texture of your clay sculpture was highly detailed. The release agent can build up into the texture impressions of the mold, preventing the foam from running into these areas and capturing the fine detail.

Preparing the Armature

After both halves of the mold have been brushed with the mold release agent, the armature must be wrapped with a material that will protect it from the corrosive effects of the hot foam (Fig. 4-3). Wrapping also prevents the foam from seeping into areas of the

armature where it isn't wanted (e.g. inside the joints).

Figure 4-3

A number of materials can be used to wrap the armature. Since the wrapping material will be part of the final animated puppet, it should be elastic and stretchable, unlike most cloth). Some good materials for wrapping armatures are prophylactics, nylon hose, and thin balloons. The wrapping material should be affixed to itself at one end with a small piece of tape, to prevent it from coming loose when the armature is reinserted into the mold cavity.

Once the armature is wrapped, it must be **repositioned** inside the mold cavity so that it is centered properly. This is a difficult task, but there is a trick that makes it easier. In the last chapter, the sculpture was suspended from the mounting board via a set of screws that went into its feet. When the mold was pulled apart, these screws were removed. The screws will now be reinserted through the third mold piece and back into the bottoms of the feet (Fig. 4-4).

Once the armature is securely anchored at the bottom of the mold (Fig. 4-5), it can be repositioned until it is suspended in the center of the mold cavity. Make sure that the arms, hands, face and chest are not touching any part of the mold. When you inject

Figure 4-4

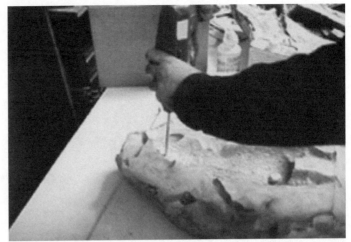

Figure 4-6

the foam into the mold cavity with the **injection gun**, the liquid foam will move into the space between the armature parts and the mold impression, and proper positioning will ensure that the armature is in the center of the final foam casting, rather than right at the surface.

Figure 4-5

Before placing the back half of the mold onto the front half, an injection hole must be drilled to accommodate the nozzle of the injection gun. The injection hole should be drilled in the back of the head of the mold cavity, where minute sculptural detail is not as critical as it is in the front on the face (Fig. 4-6). Obviously, the diameter of the drill bit must be large enough to accommodate the injection nozzle.

Securing the Mold

Close up the mold by placing the back half onto the front piece. The mold closing can and should be reinforced with **oven buckle belts** (Fig. 4-7). These are special belts that can withstand the hot temperatures of the curing process, and can be purchased from most mold-making supply centers. The belts are required to hold the mold pieces together while the foam cures in the oven. Foam expands while it cures, and without the belts, the pressure of the expanding foam will force the mold halves apart, ruining your puppet casting.

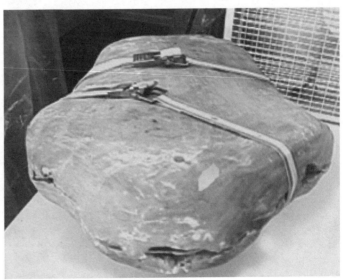

Figure 4-7

Mixing the Foam

As mentioned previously, GM Foam comes in four parts: the foaming agent, the curing agent, the gelling agent, and the foam latex base with ammonia mixture (Fig. 4-8).

Figure 4-8

The individual ingredients must be carefully mixed to achieve excellent results, and this requires paying special attention when measuring. An indispensable tool for measuring and weighing foam latex is a **gram weight scale** (Fig. 4-9).

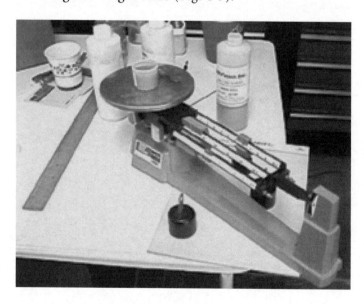

Figure 4-9

The gram weight scale is a very accurate and precise way of measuring the various components of the latex mixture. Hot foam latex must be measured

properly; improper mixing will destroy the cells that form the foam wall once it is set, resulting in substandard cell structure and foam that might tear easily. Like most types of foam, GM Foam comes with instructions for mixing it properly.

The weight scale pictured uses hanging weights to measure close weight tolerances (Fig. 4-10).

Figure 4-10

A critical requirement for foam mixing is proper room temperature, with 70 degrees or so being the optimal temperature for GM Foam.

At this point, you will need to decide on the type of electric mixer to use. The instructions for mixing GM Foam are based on the use of a heavy-duty kitchen Sunbeam Electric MixMaster (Fig. 4-11).

This mixer comes in several models, but the best one for mixing foam has 12 speeds, marked 1 through 12 on the dial (Fig. 4-12).

Figure 4-11

Figure 4-12

Like most hot foams, GM Foam should be mixed according to room temperature and humidity at that given time. The directions outlined below are for mixing hot foam at a room temperature of 69–74 degrees, for 14-½ minutes. These instructions will also be included in your foam kit.

To begin, set a large mixing bowl (which will fit onto your mixer) on the scale and zero the scale out (zeroing the scale discounts the weight of the bowl as you mix the ingredients). If your scale cannot be zeroed out, then simply factor out the weight of the bowl while mixing.

Open some doors and windows, turn on the ventilating fan and put on a facemask to keep from inhaling the foam and ammonia fumes. Pour the required amount of pure foam base into the mixing bowl (Fig. 4-13). For a 12 to 14-inch tall puppet, a mix using 150 grams of foam is usually sufficient.

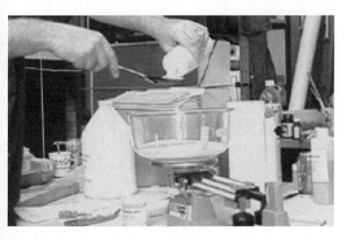

Figure 4-13

Next, add 30 grams of foaming agent, followed by 15 grams of curing agent.

Place the bowl beneath the mixer and set your kitchen timer to one minute. You can also use a stopwatch or wristwatch to keep track of the total elapsed time. Mix the components for one minute at speed #1 as marked on the mixer dial (Fig. 4-14).

Figure 4-14

After one minute, turn the dial to speed #7 and whip the mixture for six minutes. Watch the mixture carefully, and if it doesn't seem to be expanding much, add a pinch of foaming agent. Don't add too much, or it will over-foam and flow out of the mixing bowl. If you accurately measured all of the ingredients on the weight scale beforehand, you should not need to add any more.

Once this six-minute time block has elapsed, turn the dial to speed #4 and refine the mixture for three minutes.

At the end of the three minutes, reduce to speed #1 and ultra-refine for three more minutes.

Pour the gel into the mixture and mix it at speed #1 for 30 seconds.

Turn the bowl backwards (in the opposite direction of the beater rotation) by hand to mix the gel further at speed #1 for 30 more seconds.

Finally, let the mixer run at speed #1 for another 30 seconds, for a total mixing time of 14-½ minutes. Turn off the mixer and raise the beaters from the bowl.

At this point the foam is beginning to set, and you will need to work quickly. Sometimes the gel can cause the foam to set too quickly, even while you are pouring the foam mixture into the injection gun. When this happens, you need to re-mix the foam.

Figure 4-16

Injecting the Foam

With the armature now inside the mold, prop the mold so that it is standing straight up, with the injection hole at the bottom (Fig 4-15, 4-16).

Figure 4-17

Provided that you have mixed enough foam, the excess will begin to bleed out from the bleed conduits. A small amount might also bleed out along the mold seam. Most significantly, you should see foam emerge from the bottom of the feet, where the tie-down screws are (Fig. 4-18).

Figure 4-15

Pour the mixture into the injection gun, place the nozzle of the gun into the injection hole, and gently, but firmly, push the plunger, forcing the foam into the mold cavity (Fig. 4-17).

Figure 4-18

It is crucial that you see foam come from the bottom of the feet, because this will indicate that the foam has gone all the way to the bottom of the mold cavity. Foam seeping from any nooks and crannies of the mold seam is also a good indicator that the mold cavity has been completely filled. Of course, one cannot be certain until the mold is pried apart and the casting inspected. Sometimes, the tip of a nose or finger has an air pocket, which leaves a hole in that appendage. This is another reason why it is important to carve small bleed conduits (see Fig. 3-49), to allow air inside the mold to escape.

After the foam has been injected into the mold, remove the nozzle. To prevent any foam from seeping out through the injection hole, plug it with a piece of clay (Fig. 4-19).

Figure 4-19

Leave the mold upright for at least 15 to 20 minutes, to allow the foam to further gel inside.

Curing the Foam

The mold can now be placed in a curing oven. A curing oven has a fan that circulates the heat, keeping the temperature consistent and the hot air flowing around the mold. A conventional kitchen gas or electric oven does not work well, because they shut on and off periodically, and thus do not provide a consistent temperature around the mold and throughout the curing process. It is also not a good practice to use a kitchen oven for baking foam because the foam

releases toxic fumes. Curing ovens have a port that attaches to a flexible pipe conduit running from the oven port to a window, allowing the fumes to escape the room. Most foam companies can help you locate a curing oven.

The mold should now be placed inside the oven and baked at 185 degrees for approximately three hours. However, the rat puppet described in this chapter represented a curious anomaly. Since the fingers of the palm were wire, they needed to be affixed to the armature's palm with **epoxy putty**. This particular epoxy could only withstand heat of 125 degrees F; baking the mold at the regular temperature would have destroyed the epoxy. Since the mold had to be baked at 125 degrees, the baking time had to be increased. At the lower temperature, it was necessary to bake the mold for nine hours. Normally one does not come across such a situation, and the standard procedure will be used.

Once the baking is finished, the mold is removed from the oven and allowed to cool overnight. After it has cooled, the belts can be removed (Fig. 4-20).

Figure 4-20

A simple wooden stick, pointed at one end (Fig. 4-21), can now be used to pry up one half of the mold.

Go around the perimeter of the mold and insert the pry stick into the keys, gently forcing the mold halves apart. Eventually the halves will loosen enough to take them apart and reveal the foam casting

Figure 4-21

inside. The tie-downs can now be removed from the feet (Fig. 4-22).

Figure 4-22

Removing the Foam Casting

Notice that the casting has foam webbing between the arms and legs, and around the head and ears (Fig. 4-22, 4-23, 4-25).

This is called **flashing**, and is the result of foam seeping out of the mold cavity and flowing between the mold halves during the injection process. This can be removed easily with a pair of scissors once the casting is removed from the mold. The immediate problem is how to remove the casting itself from the mold half. The casting must be removed very slowly, or the foam may tear. Using your fingers, gently pull

Figure 4-23

the sides of the casting away from the mold wall (Fig. 4-24). Go around the entire perimeter of the casting, gently prying the fingers, sides, toes, legs, arms, ears, and head, until everything is loosened.

Figure 4-24

Continue pulling and prying the casting until you work it free of the mold (Fig. 4-25). The flashing will now be quite evident.

Figure 4-25

CLEANING UP THE PUPPET

To get rid of the latex odor of the casting, run water over the casting and squeeze the rubber, gently wringing it out like a sponge. Make certain that ALL of the water has been squeezed from the casting before painting it. Let the casting air dry overnight, or place it in a warm curing oven for an hour or so, to evaporate any remaining moisture. This water treatment will also clean the surface, allowing the paints to be absorbed into the pores of the casting more effectively.

With a sharp pair of scissors, cut the flashing from the casting, being very careful not to cut into the side of the puppet. If you do (and provided that the result is not a gaping hole), you can patch the hole with liquid latex base. In fact, once the casting is removed, you will notice any places where air pockets formed holes on the surface of the casting. These can be patched using the latex and a small brush (Fig. 4-26, 4-27).

Figure 4-28

Figure 4-26

The finished casting (Fig. 4-28).

Figure 4-27

Painting the Foam Puppet

THE IMPORTANCE OF PAINT TYPE

The puppet can now be painted. Theories abound as to what types of paints to use. Since the puppet will need to be posed for single-frame animation, the paint used must be treated so that it becomes, to some extent, rubberized. The author has used acrylic-based paints to good effect, but occasionally acrylics will crack. One must remember that an animation puppet will need to *move* during single-frame animation. If the proper measures are not taken when painting the puppet, movement of the joints will cause cracking to occur in the paint, destroying not only the paint job, but the illusion of life as well. There must be an intermediary substance between the foam and the paint; namely, an adhesive which will both stick to the surface of the foam and provide a tacky surface for the paint to adhere to. To further keep the paint from cracking, the paint itself must (to some degree) be absorbed into the porous surface of the foam. Two products can be used for this purpose.

One is called Prosthetic Adhesive, and it can be purchased through Grand Stage Lighting in Chicago,

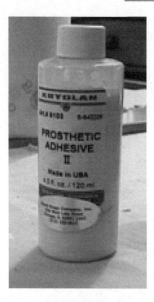

Figure 4-29

Illinois. The other is Prose-Aid, another liquid adhesive, sold by ADM Tronics Unlimited of North Vale, New Jersey. To paint our rat puppet we will be using Prosthetic Adhesive II (Fig. 49).

PAINTING TECHNIQUE

This product is a kind of glue that leaves a tacky surface once it has dried. Straight from the bottle, the adhesive may be too thick to apply to the casting's surface. The adhesive should be brushed onto the surface of the casting in a thin coat, and it can be thinned by adding a bit of ammonia. The ammonia helps the adhesive to be absorbed by the foam, and it eventually evaporates.

After the first coat of adhesive has been brushed on, we will next apply a thin coat of paint. A good paint for this purpose is a product called **Universal Colorant**, which is available at most art supply shops. It comes in a wide variety of colors. The paint should be brushed onto the casting surface in a light coat. Once this coat dries, apply another thin coat of the adhesive/ammonia mixture, followed by another coat of paint. Continue doing this until at least four coats of each have been applied. Building up the coats in layers will significantly minimize any possible paint cracking during animation. The layers will also hide the original color of the foam casting.

After the puppet casting has been painted, it must be treated with something to get rid of the tacky surface left by the adhesive and paints. Cornstarch is a simple yet very effective remedy for this problem. It is colorless and leaves no stain on the puppet. A small brush (such as an ox brush) can be used to brush on the cornstarch. This needs to be done quickly, because the puppet surface, while still tacky, will begin collecting dust, dirt, and anything else airborne or on your fingers. Any residual cornstarch can be removed with a small airbrush or hair dryer.

The finished, painted puppet (Fig. 4-30).

Figure 4-30

Manufacture of Eyes and Eyeballs

There are a number of ways to create and animate eyes for puppets. One process involves a large plastic bead with a hole in the center. The bead is painted white (to suggest the eyeball itself), and the center hole is painted black (to infer the dark pupil). A pointed object can then be inserted into the hole and the eyeball moved about during the animation process. The eyeballs of many of the puppets built by Aardman Animations—the creators of Wallace and Gromit animated shorts, as well as the stop-motion feature film, *Chicken Run* (2000)—are animated by using this technique.

A simpler and faster method is to take a sphere

(such as a marble or a plastic sphere) and paint it white. Once dried, this sphere is popped into the eye socket of the puppet, and Vaseline is brushed onto the eyeball. A piece of black clay is formed into a pupil, and then placed onto the surface of the eyeball. Since the clay is resting on the Vaseline, it can easily be moved about on the eyeball sphere, and will not slip off. Another advantage of this method is that Vaseline has a glistening sheen to it, suggesting the wet surface of an eye. When studio lights hit the eye surface, the result is a very naturalistic eye appearance. Stop-motion/cgi animator Thomas R. Smith (*Dinosaur,* [2000]; *The P.J.s* [1999]), has used this technique to very good effect, as have a number of other animators.

CHAPTER 5

Creating Build-Up Puppets

A Cursory History of the Art

As its name implies, the **build-up technique** requires the sculptor to form (or build up) either the musculature or skin textures of the character, or both, directly over the armature, using pieces of foam, rubber or some other type of flexible material. The build-up technique was the precursor of foam injection. Stop-motion puppets made at the turn of the twentieth century were often fabricated as quickly and as easily as possible, from a wide variety of materials. Many of the puppets of master Russian animator Ladislaw Starevitch (1892–1965), were created in this fashion. In particular, his film *The Mascot* (1934) utilized puppets that were built from glass, wood, cloth, and wire. The foam injection process took many years to perfect, and it was much more common for animators to simply build up puppets from everyday found objects and materials. For the RKO motion picture *Mighty Joe Young* (1949), sculptor Marcel Delgado, who had previously worked for visual effects pioneer Willis O'Brien on *King Kong* (1933), developed a build-up technique that was intended for the Joe Young puppets. The process proved rather labor-intensive, and was ultimately abandoned in favor of foam injection.

The build-up technique has an advantage over foam injection in that considerable realism can be achieved when it is executed properly. This is because the muscles are literally built up over the skeletal armature framework. When the armature is moved about, the muscles will flex, contract, and move in a fashion similar to the muscles of a real person or creature. Because of this, detailed anatomy is critical when executing the process. One of the finest examples of build-up technique for a stop-motion model used in a feature film is of the Chasmosaur dinosaur from the Hammer Films production, *When Dinosaurs Ruled the Earth* (1970). Built and animated by Jim Danforth, the puppet's appearance and performance are extremely realistic.

O'Brien's protégé, visual effects creative artist Ray Harryhausen, would develop a body of feature film work unparalleled in the history of stop-motion animation effects. Most of the models used in Harryhausen's films were fabricated using foam injection techniques. A notable exception, however, was his use of the build-up process to sculpt the seven sword-yielding human skeletons in the Columbia Pictures fantasy film, *Jason and the Argonauts* (1963). For these models, Harryhausen had his father, Fred Harryhausen (a machinist by trade) tool the seven armatures. These armatures were shipped to Ray in England, where he used a mixture of latex and cotton to build up the bones of the skeletons directly over the armatures. The surfaces of the bones were smoothed out with a few coats of thin latex applied with a brush, and the models were painted.

This chapter will outline the procedure for building up foam muscles and detailed latex skin appliances, in this case while creating a puppet of a Greek mythological creature, the Minotaur. The

47

muscles of the puppet will be as detailed as possible, in order to create a realistic, yet stylized, appearance.

Research

Research is crucial when creating a lifelike puppet, and the Minotaur was no exception. To aid in the initial design stages of sculpting the Minotaur over the armature, it was necessary to consult works both on the art of ancient Greece and general anatomy. The author chose as a point of departure two books to aid him in the initial design stages: *Ancient Greece*, and *Gray's Anatomy*. The local library is an invaluable resource for this kind of research, and should satisfy most of your requirements.

In the early design stages, it is usually best to go directly to the source (in this case an image of a bull's head), rather than to rely on memory (Fig. 5-1). Even in a classroom setting, many students do not take the time to research when designing their own characters. Creating and maintaining a **morgue file** will ensure that the creative artist always has an ample supply of research material on hand when undertaking another endeavor.

While research can involve a wide range of sources, perhaps the greatest danger is that one can come to rely on a particular look, rather than on one's own imagination. It is crucial that the designer keep in mind the fact that the final appearance of the puppet should complement the unfolding story. The Minotaur needed to look like a muscular man, albeit 14 feet tall and with the head of a bull. Since the Minotaur was a bloodthirsty and violent beast, the author elected to make the puppet rather stocky and broad across the shoulders and chest, as well as in the neck area. This would help to make the Minotaur appear quite strong and difficult (if not impossible) to vanquish (Fig. 5-2, 5-3).

Figure 5-2 and 5-3

The Application of Foam Pieces Onto the Metal Armature

The following illustrations will outline the build-up process for creating foam muscles from pieces of foam padding and mixed foam latex skins. In theory, the process is relatively simple: all one needs is the armature (either machined or wire), a slab of foam rubber, a pair of sharp scissors, specialized cement glue, hot foam for the skin, a few sculpting tools and paints.

PREPARING THE ARMATURE

First, the armature (if it is machined) must be properly tightened before it is covered. This tightening

Figure 5-1

is really dependent on the personal preference of the animator: some animators prefer very tight armatures, while others prefer armatures that are easier to manipulate with little struggle. The joints must be tightened to the preferred tension before the armature is covered. The armature is then placed in a generic **"Da Vinci" pose**. The Da Vinci pose, named after a well-known drawing by Leonardo da Vinci (Fig. 5-4), is a neutral position for the armature to be in while one proceeds with the sculpture (Fig. 5-5, 5-6).

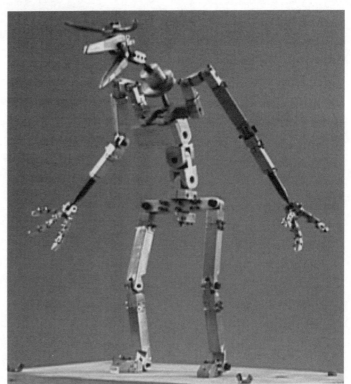

Figure 5-5

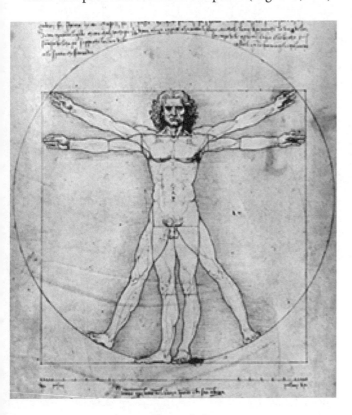

Figure 5-4

The knees and elbows are slightly bent, and the spine slightly curved forward. The rule of thumb is to place the armature in the position that the puppet will be in when it is at rest. This resting pose helps to give the puppet its character and personality. Note in Fig. 5-3 that the Minotaur is bent slightly forward, due to its large upper back (one characteristic of a bull's back). Since the back is bent in this way, the armature must be bent in like fashion. Another reason that the knees and elbows are bent slightly is so that when the muscles are attached to the armature, they will, in effect, be placed in a halfway flexed pose, and will hence flex more realistically when the limbs are fully extended or contracted.

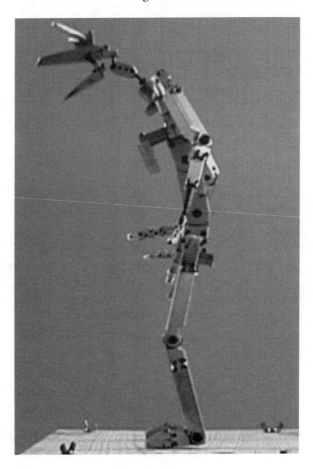

Figure 5-6

Blocking Out the Figure in Foam

Once the armature is positioned correctly, the next step is to settle upon a glue to affix the foam muscle pieces to the armature surface. Not just any glue will work, as metal has a very slick, smooth surface to which most glue will not adhere well. Indeed, since the muscles will need to flex and contract, the glue chosen must also have some degree of elasticity built into its makeup. One might consider the glue to function as a tendon would (tendons are tough, cordlike, dense tissues that connect a muscle with a bone surface). Epoxy putty would therefore be a poor choice, because once it sets, it is extremely hard, has no elasticity, and does not grab particularly well onto a smooth, slick surface like metal. An excellent choice for gluing foam pieces onto a metallic surface (as well as to other foam pieces) is a product called Barge (Fig. 5-7), which is a type of rubber cement glue manufactured by Quabaug Corporation, in North Brookfield, Massachusetts. Barge can be found at most Ace Hardware stores, or it can be purchased in bulk from Quabaug. This may be the better choice, particularly if one is planning to use the build-up technique exclusively, because a lot of Barge is needed to glue pieces together, and the tubes are about two fluid ounces.

The next item necessary for the build-up technique is a block of foam (Fig. 5-8). This is the same flexible **polyurethane foam** that is often used in mattresses and pillows. There are different types of polyurethane foam (or polymer types, which are soft or rigid), so try and find the type that springs back easily when pinched. This foam can often be found at a fabrics shop.

Figure 5-8

You will also need a pair of sharp scissors (Fig. 5-10). Again, a nice, sharp pair can be found where you would find the foam. Two pairs of scissors are ideal for cutting and shaping the foam pieces: a large pair for the initial cutting of the large block, and a smaller pair for cutting detail and forming the final muscle shape.

Figure 5-7

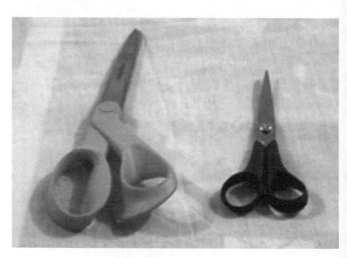

Figure 5-9

For this demonstration, we will begin at the lower extremities of the puppet, and work our way up the armature. No two people work in exactly the same way when sculpting; some people work their way up, some work down, some skip here and there. It's a personal choice, often determined by how one's creative process works. As you develop your sculpting style, you will learn what process best suits you.

We will begin with the lower legs, and cut pieces for the gastronemicus (calf) muscles and lower leg muscles. Use the large pair of scissors to cut an initial slab of foam (Fig. 5-10). Consult the anatomical book you will be using to determine the proper proportions for the height, length, and girth of the muscle you are sculpting.

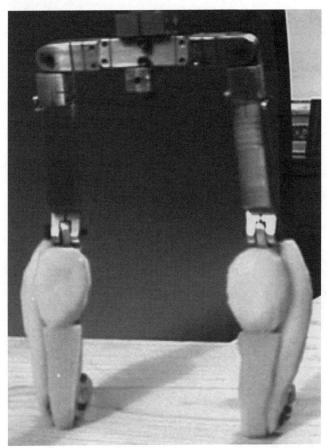

Figure 5-11

Figure 5-10

Dab some of the Barge onto the surface of the armature where the muscle will be placed, then dab some on the foam piece itself. Wait for the two surfaces to dry and press them together onto the armature (Fig. 5-11). This is called a **dry mount**. Barge has a tacky surface once it is dried, and since both surfaces will be tacky, they will bond to one another. NOTE: This glue works extremely well — too well, actually. Therefore, you must make certain that you position the muscle exactly where you want it on the armature. Otherwise, it will be nearly impossible to remove the foam without destroying it, and you will need to remove residual glue from the armature surface with an X-Acto or utility knife.

Continue up the legs with the quadriceps (thigh) muscles (Fig. 5-12).

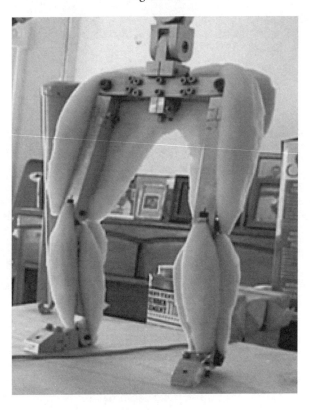

Figure 5-12

Proceed with the attachment of the inside leg muscles (Fig. 5-13). Muscles that traverse from one bone to another are attached at their ends, from one bone to the other. In the case of the inside leg muscles, note how one end of the muscle is attached to the bottom of the pelvic area, while the other end is attached near the knee. This theory of muscle placement and proper attachment will serve you well when you are animating the puppet, because it will allow the muscles to flex and bend over other muscles in a realistic fashion, mimicking their behavior in real life.

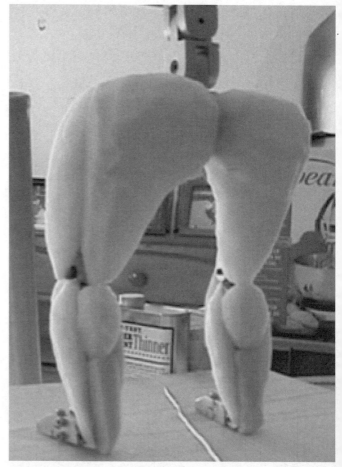

Figure 5-14

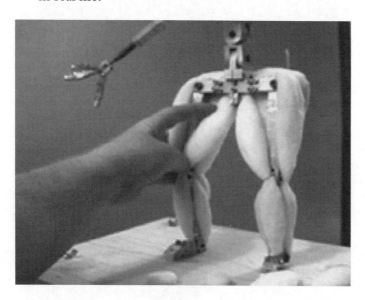

Figure 5-13

At this juncture, there are quite a few muscles on the legs, so it is a good idea to rotate the model around and begin constructing the backside. Begin by forming pieces that will represent the glutei (buttocks) muscles (Fig. 5-14).

Once the legs have been blocked out, cut a large piece of foam for the abdominal wall (Fig. 5-15).

Notice that the abdomen is begun in the front, rather than by taking a huge piece of foam and wrapping it around the entire spine section (front, back, and sides). As you attach muscles, carefully observe how real muscles are attached, layered, and overlapped. If you duplicate this natural phenomenon when building your puppet, a much more naturalistic appearance will result.

Notice that no surface detail has yet been applied to the foam pieces. Later in this chapter we will

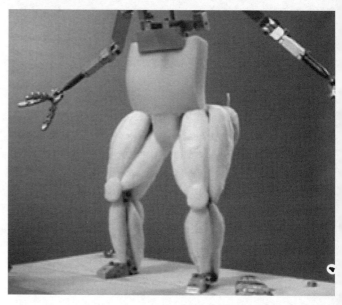

Figure 5-15

apply a thick sheet of air-cured foam latex (with textured detail), which will be wrapped around the muscles.

Continue by forming the pectoral (chest), deltoid (shoulder), and bicep (forearm) muscles (Fig. 5-16).

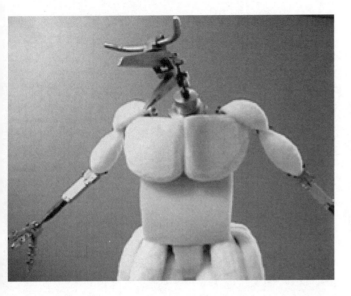

Figure 5-16

Next, begin shaping the muscles for the forearm (Fig. 5-17). Polyurethane foam is not easy to cut, which is why it is a good idea to form the muscle with a sharp pair of scissors. The scissors take a lot of abuse, and the author will often invest in a new pair of scissors when creating a new puppet.

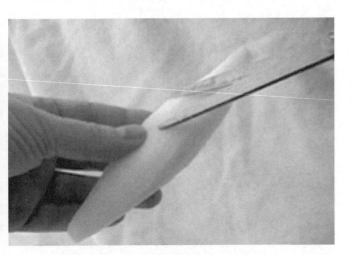

Figure 5-17

Apply a liberal amount of Barge glue to the armature, and then to the surface of the foam muscle you have just formed (Fig. 5-18).

Do the same for the other side of the arm (Fig. 5-19).

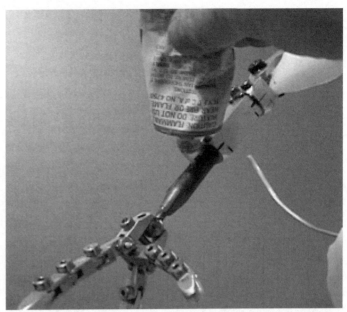

Figure 5-18

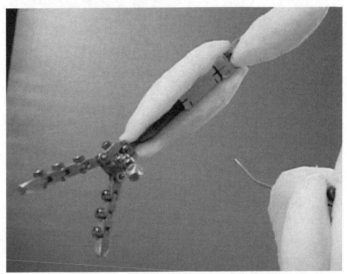

Figure 5-19

Figure 5-20

Attach a foam muscle next to the center of the arm (Fig. 5-21), making sure that all arm muscles begin at the elbow and then link into the top of the wrist. Once the glue on these muscles has dried, you can test the crossing of the arm muscles by turning the joint of the forearm longitudinally. Note in Fig. 5-21 that the muscles overlap in the forearm, as they do in real life. If you pay careful attention to how muscles are shaped and layered, your puppet's musculature will appear quite lifelike in its movements when animated.

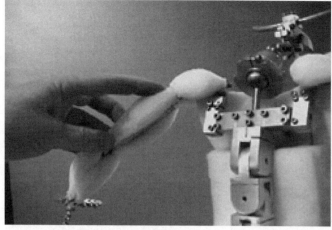

Figure 5-22

Figure 5-21

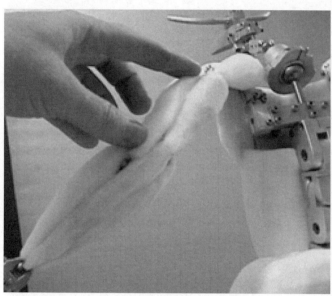

Figure 5-23

Turn the puppet around and begin attaching muscles in the back of the arm. Cut a piece for the tricep (back of upper arm) muscle, and glue it into place (Fig. 5-22).

Now layer a muscle for the side of the upper arm (Fig. 5-23).

Finally, place a muscle on the inside of the upper arm (Fig. 5-24).

We will now apply the muscles of the back. In the case of this Minotaur puppet, the author did not wish to exactly copy every muscle of the human body, and opted instead to stylize the puppet. The style of the film in which the puppet would be appearing required not that the Minotaur look absolutely

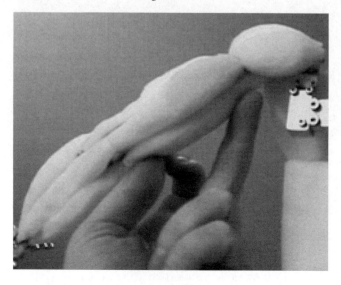

Figure 5-24

real, but that it resemble art figures on ancient Greek vases, jars, and frescos. Because of this creative decision, the author chose to simply block the back muscles out with two large pieces of foam that represent the latissimus dorsi (back) muscles (Fig. 5-25). These are large, triangular-shaped muscles that form the shape of the upper (and to some degree middle) back. They attach to the shoulder area, and to the lower portion of the spine.

We now run into a curious situation that arises when dealing with the build-up technique. In most foam-injected puppets, the armature is entirely covered with foam, so that no large cavities exist inside the puppet. With a built-up puppet, however, this is not always the case. By going around the perimeter of the armature's torso and applying blocks of muscle accordingly, we have created some space inside the torso cavity (Fig. 5-27).

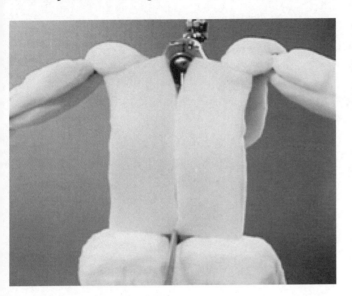

Figure 5-25

Finish the back area by forming and attaching the trapezium (two triangular-shaped muscles between the neck and shoulders) at the bottom of the neck (Fig. 5-26).

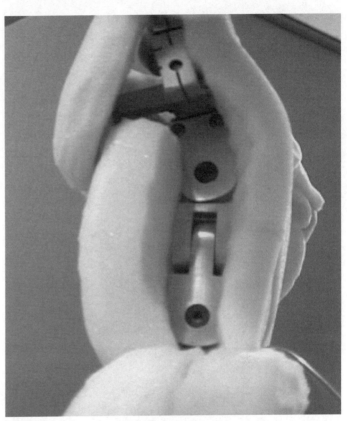

Figure 5-27

Generally, this is not a critical issue, but if one wishes, the space can be filled by placing cotton balls or small foam pieces inside the cavity. The author prefers cotton balls, because they have some degree of squash and stretch, are odorless, and do not need to be shaped with scissors, which expedites the sculpting process. Place cotton balls in the outside cavity of the torso, and anywhere else you feel the sculpture might need it (Fig. 5-28).

The sides can now be closed up with strips of foam, cut to shape along the sides of the torso (Fig. 5-29, 5-30).

Reinforce the join of the side muscle with that

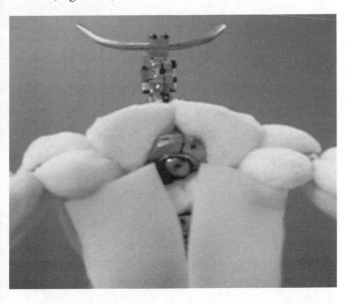

Figure 5-26

Figure 5-28

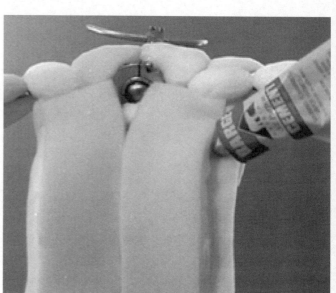

Figure 5-30

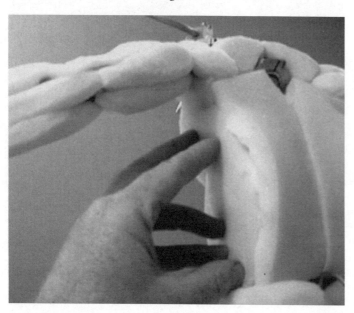

Figure 5-29

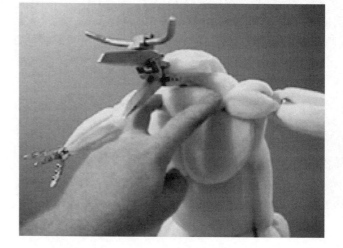

Figure 5-31

of the latissimus muscles, using more Barge (Fig. 5-31).

Cover the space between the chest and trapezium muscles with a small block of foam (Fig. 5-32).

Since the design calls for the Minotaur to have a heavy, hump back, a large foam piece is formed and placed down the center of the back, beginning at the base of the neck, and ending about mid-spine (Fig. 5-33).

Figure 5-32

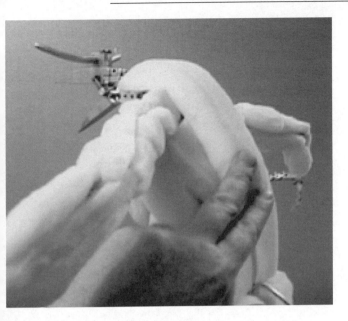

Figure 5-33

With the exception of the fingers, hands, and head (which will be covered with castings of mixed foam latex), the Minotaur puppet is now blocked out with pieces of polyurethane foam (Fig. 5-34).

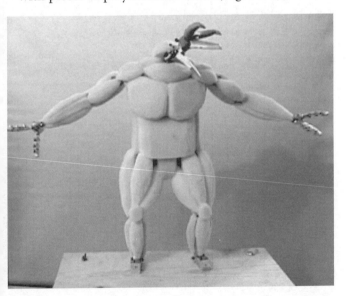

Figure 5-34

Using Epoxy Putty for Build-up Puppets

Before we proceed with the creation of the outer foam latex skin, the horns must be made. Since real horns are hard and inflexible, we won't be using foam for this part of the puppet. To give them a realistic appearance, we must sculpt them from a hard substance, specifically, a two-part epoxy putty (Fig. 5-35). Because of its extreme hardness, this type of putty is ideal for horns, teeth, eyes, chitinous surfaces, claws, or anything that does not need to flex. Two-part epoxy putty should be available in any hardware store. Make certain that it is putty, and not **resin**. Resin is a free-flowing liquid epoxy, while epoxy putty has the consistency of clay, and can be easily formed into the desired shape.

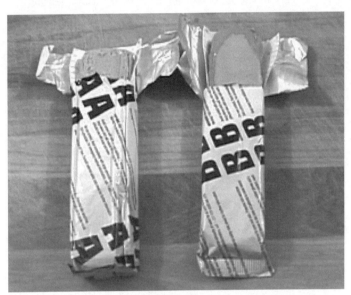

Figure 5-35

Most epoxies will come with mixing instructions, but generally the mixtures require equal parts of the hardener and the resin (Fig. 5-36).

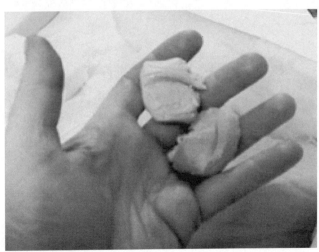

Figure 5-36

The Minotaur armature pictured was machined with two aluminum horns. These aluminum horn pieces act as an understructure around which to form the putty. Equal parts of the resin and hardener should be mixed into a ball until it is a uniform color. Epoxy putty must be mixed correctly or it will not set properly. If there are streaks in the putty, it has not been mixed sufficiently. Working times vary from putty to putty, but generally, half an hour is enough to mix the putty, then form it into the desired shapes. The putty is soft when it is first mixed, but as it hardens, it will become more manageable. The nice thing about epoxy putty is that it can be added to, scraped away, filed, drilled, and cut with a Dremel tool. The putty is next formed around the aluminum horns (Fig. 5-37), and then smoothed out (Fig. 5-38). Detail can be added (such as chips, indentations, or scoring) by sculpting them into the putty before it hardens.

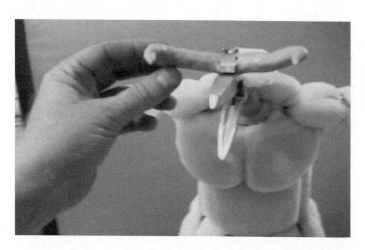

Figure 5-37

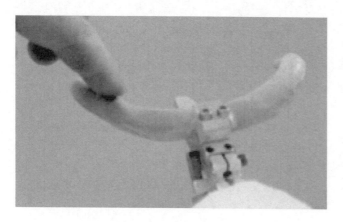

Figure 5-38

Casting a Latex Skin

Now that the general shape of the puppet has been formed around the armature, the next step is to create a thin skin, complete with textures. This skin will be wrapped around the muscles of the puppet, giving the puppet a realistic skin texture. The skin will be cast in foam from an Ultracal mold. The mold must be large enough to cast skin piece of sufficient size to be pulled and cut to the shape of the various muscled areas of the puppet. A large surface is required to begin the mold process. A large cutting board will suffice (Fig. 5-39).

Figure 5-39

THE CLAY FORM

Roma clay, which comes in blocks, will be used to lay down a surface (Fig. 5-40). Skin detail will then be sculpted into the clay surface.

Figure 5-40

Since the board must be completely covered, it is best to cut thin, more manageable strips of clay from the blocks (Fig. 5-41), and lay the clay down in pieces onto the board (Fig. 5-42).

Figure 5-43

ered with fingerprint impressions. To clean it up, smooth everything out with a curved tool, for example a spoon (Fig. 5-44).

Figure 5-41

Figure 5-44

Detail can now be added to the surface of the clay. The detail will depend primarily on the character of the puppet. For our Minotaur, we will sculpt a skin that is somewhat bumpy, with a few wrinkles. Other details (such as folds of skin and a leathery texture) will be added later, after the foam latex pieces are applied to the muscles. The puppet still needs some sort of abdominal muscles; those muscles will now be sculpted into the clay (Fig. 5-45).

Once the muscles are shaped, a bumpy, wrinkled texture can be sculpted onto the surface (Fig. 5-46).

When the clay impression is finished, a mold wall should be erected to trap the Ultracal when it is poured over the clay (Fig. 5-47).

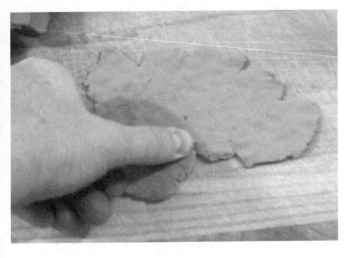

Figure 5-42

Eventually, the entire board should be covered in a thin layer of clay (Fig. 5-43).

The clay surface will be rather lumpy, and cov-

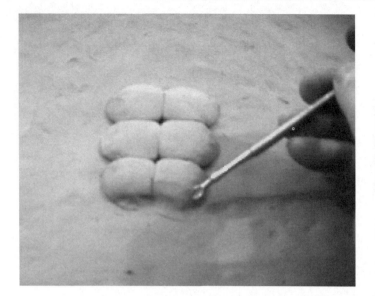

Figure 5-45

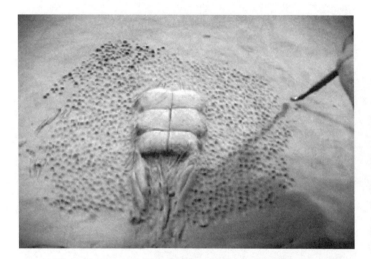

Figure 5-46

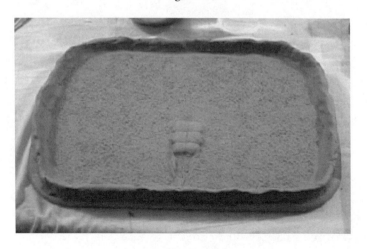

Figure 5-47

POURING THE SKIN MOLD

Mix the Ultracal and pour it into the cavity (Fig. 5-48). Allow it to set overnight.

Figure 5-48

The following day, you can remove the Ultracal mold from the clay (Fig. 5-49).

Figure 5-49

We now have a reverse mold impression of the original clay skin detail (Fig. 5-50).

Now that we have fabricated this Ultracal skin mold, we can repeatedly run foam latex skins until we have enough to cover the puppet.

Figure 5-50

Running the Foam Skin

To create foam skins, foam latex must be mixed in a blender, in the same basic fashion as when we mixed the foam for the injection process. The only difference is that the foam will not be injected, but poured onto the surface of the skin mold. This process is sometimes referred to as **slush casting**, though that term (as applied to this process) is a tad misleading. Slush casting generally refers to the process of taking foam latex (or straight latex) and pouring it into a mold cavity by hand. The mold is then rocked back and forth, allowing the foam to flow into the nooks and crannies of the mold. Once dried, the casting is removed. This process is often used to make life masks (such as Halloween masks) as a duplicate run, mass producing the same mask as quickly as possible. For our purposes, we will be mixing up a small batch of foam latex, but then we will pour this latex over the skin mold, slushing it with our hands to make the skin as thin as possible.

First, brush a liberal coating or two of mold release agent onto the textured surface of the mold.

If you recall, foam latex, when beaten, expands in size to nearly four or five times its original volume. We will not need nearly that much for our skin castings. Therefore, mix up half a batch of foam latex (Fig. 5-51).

Now pour some of this mixture over the skin mold (Fig. 5-52), smoothing it out to a thin layer with your hands.

Let this air-dry for 15 or 20 minutes. Drying time may vary depending on how much of the am-

Figure 5-51

Figure 5-52

monia base evaporated during the mixing, and the temperature of your work area. Test for adequately air-set foam by feeling its texture. If it springs back a bit, then it is ready to be removed from the mold. Care must be taken when handling the fresh foam casting, because it will still be quite soft. This softness is very important, because it will allow the sculptor to add even more detail to the skin while it is setting after it has been applied to the puppet.

Additional skins can be made from residual foam by pouring it onto a smooth, clean surface, such as a piece of glass (Fig. 5-53). Latex peels quite easily from this surface. However, for safety reasons, make certain that the pane of glass is held securely within a metal or wood frame.

Figure 5-53

The foam can then be smoothed out into an even layer across the glass, by placing a paper towel onto the foam, and then using one's hand to smooth the surface (Fig. 5-54).

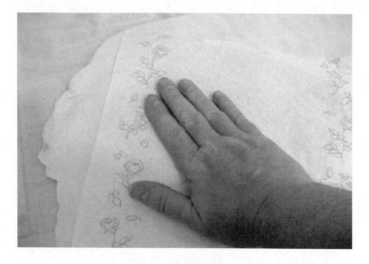

Figure 5-54

While the foam skins that have been pulled from the Ultracal mold slab have texture and detail, texture has not yet been added to the foam skins that are on the glass. The skins (whether they came off the glass or from the mold) have not yet been baked and are still soft. Because they are soft, the skins can be wrapped around the puppet, and further details added by using sculpting tools. Alternately, the skins can first be sculpted with detail and cured in an oven at a low temperature (125 degrees or so) for about two hours. When they are removed and cooled, the skins are then set and will not lose their detail, and can be applied to the puppet. However, since they are cured, one cannot sculpt further detail into them. The process described below will be based on skins that have not yet been cured (baked). Detail will be sculpted into the skins once the puppet is finished, and then the puppet will be placed into the oven and baked at a low temperature for 1.5 to 2 hours.

Applying the Latex Skin

With the scissors, cut a portion of the foam casting large enough to cover the abdomen and the crotch (Fig. 5-55).

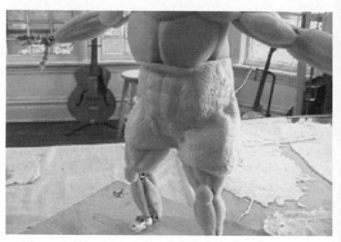

Figure 5-55

Latex castings have a certain amount of surface moisture that needs to be wiped off with a paper towel before the application of Barge, or the Barge may not adhere to the foam surfaces. If one is not in a hurry, the foam wrappings can be air-dried in a day or two.

Make sure that the seam stops at the center of the puppet's side (Fig. 5-56), preferably in the *inside* of the appendage. It is a good practice to place the seams or joins of the latex skins in these areas, where they are less likely to be detected by the audience.

Wrap one of the biceps and hide the seam underneath the arm (Fig. 5-56). Once this is done, you will begin to notice that the contours of the polyurethane foam muscles that you sculpted with the scissors and affixed to the armature show up beneath the foam skins, creating a natural-looking anatomy.

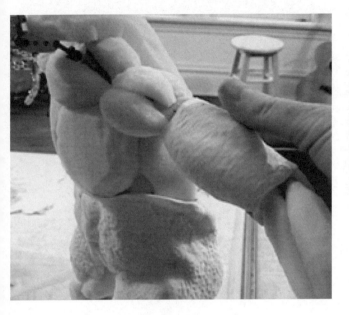

Figure 5-56

Do the same for the chest (Fig. 5-57), placing the seam at the side of the torso.

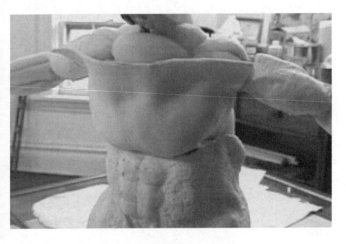

Figure 5-57

Now wrap the arms, making sure that the joins go underneath the arm. As you apply the skins, try and follow the contours of the foam muscles. This will allow the form of the muscles to show underneath the skin, giving the surface texture added detail. This also means that the skin castings must be as thin as possible, but not so thin that they will tear easily.

Cover the back and neck (Fig. 5-58).

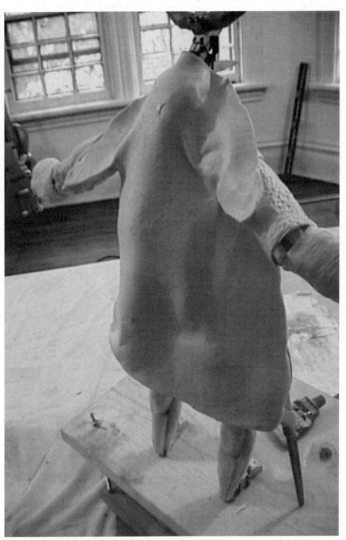

Figure 5-58

Affix some skin wrapping to the palms (Fig. 5-59).

As you prepare the wrappings for the fingers, you may want to wrap each segment of the finger (top, middle and bottom) individually. Or, you can wrap it with one piece of skin, then sculpt detail into the foam.

Make skins for the legs, and wrap them about the lower and upper portions of each leg.

In the case of this particular puppet, the last thing to be sculpted is the head. A block of cured hot foam will be placed onto the armature portion of the head and the detail sculpted out (Fig. 5-60).

Figure 5-59

Once the head has been detailed and the rest of the foam skins applied to the muscles, the model should be air-dried for two or more days. Keep in mind that during this time, the skin will still be soft

Figure 5-61

reflect light, he opted to use stainless steel bearings (Fig. 5-62).

Figure 5-60

enough that you can sculpt more detail into it, but that option disappears once the skins have dried.

The Finishing Touches

The author machined two cloven hooves for the Minotaur's feet, and bolted them to the feet of the puppet (Fig. 5-61).

You can now paint the model in your preferred **color scheme**, using the same technique (described in Chapter Four) that is used for painting a foam-injected puppet.

Once the model has been painted, you can then add surface detail and finishing touches. Our Minotaur puppet will need eyes, teeth, and hair. Since the author wanted the puppet's eyes to appear lifeless and

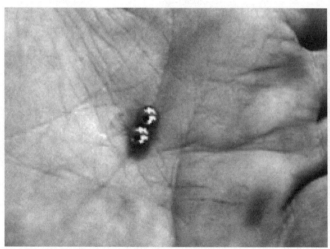

Figure 5-62

Placing the bearings into the sockets of the eyes gives the puppet a detached, unfeeling and cold facial expression (Fig. 5-63a and b).

To create teeth, epoxy putty was rolled into the shapes of tusks and pointed teeth, and then superglued

Figure 5-63a

Figure 5-63b

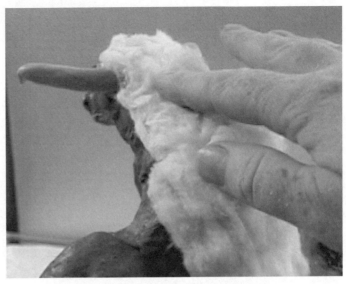

Figure 5-65

into place in the gums of the open mouth (Fig. 5-65a).

The author chose to give the Minotaur a hairy back and chest. A number of materials would have served the purpose, but ordinary cotton was selected to simplify the matter. The cotton balls were rolled out (Fig. 5-64).

Figure 5-64

Figure 5-66

Prose Aid or Prosthetic Adhesive can be painted onto the back of the model, and then the cotton strands pressed into the back, securing them in place (Fig. 5-65).

Hair was next added to the chest (Fig. 5-66).

The finished built-up puppet appears in Fig. 5-67.

Figure 5-67

Concluding Remarks

The reader is now acquainted with the two fundamental processes for creating a stop-motion animation puppet. It must be noted, however, that there are many variants of these processes. Often, a foam-injected model may be built up with additional skin pieces to create a final surface texture. Conversely, a built-up model may utilize pre-cast foam-injected pieces to supplement its final appearance. There is really no right or wrong way. Whatever the technique, it is imperative that one be well acquainted with anatomy, including bone structure, muscle layering and flexing, and the details of how muscles move beneath the skin. A person who does not have a firm grasp of these physiological principles will have considerable difficulty creating a convincing-looking model.

This manual has explained how to create puppets using both oven-cured and sheet foam, but the choice of materials need not stop there. As mentioned earlier, the great Russian puppet animator, Ladislaw Starevitch, used a multitude of materials to create his puppets: foam, cloth, wood, glass, paper, and anything else that he felt would serve his purpose. One is limited only by the depth of one's own imagination, and the level of experience garnered using various construction materials. In the Paramount Pictures film *The Golden Child* (1986), there is a stop-motion sequence in which a mysterious young boy magically brings to life an aluminum soft drink can, which subsequently does a dance to the tune of "Puttin' on the Ritz." Since aluminum cans are quite thin and easily cut and bent, animator Tom St.

Amand chose to use a real soft drink can for the animation. When one can became worn out from the many frames of animation, he simply substituted a fresh one, repeating the process as shooting progressed. The sequence is wonderfully animated and quite fun to watch, and since St. Amand was using actual cans, they looked completely real. In the Columbia Pictures film *Mysterious Island* (1961), a giant crab menaces a group of shipwrecked American Civil War soldiers on a deserted island. To create the puppet, animator Ray Harryhausen used an actual crab shell, into which was placed a machined armature. The crab appears real because it is a real crab shell. The illusion is quite startling.

Working with foam is just one technique used in the art of creating animation puppets, so do not be misled into thinking that foam is the only material to use. As you gain experience, you will discover that there are hundreds, if not thousands of materials at your disposal for the creation and manufacture of puppets. It may even behoove an animator to seek out the advice and experience of a marionette puppeteer, preferably one who has worked in puppetry for many years. You may discover that people outside of the film animation realm, who do live-performance puppetry, have considerable knowledge of materials used to create puppets that can possibly be used in the animation arena.

As you continue to develop your skills in puppet animation and puppet fabrication, your preferences for technique and material are of course a matter of personal choice. In the final analysis, the audience will only remember their reaction to your work of art and judge it by how deeply it affected them. If you create something that has been seen before and does not have a particularly fresh appearance, there may be little response from the viewer. If, on the other hand, your idea is fresh, compelling, and thought provoking, the result may be something that is worth watching and talking about for years to come.

Finally, some artists take themselves and their work too seriously, and expect everyone else to do the same. Have something meaningful to say, but don't forget to have fun doing so! Enjoying yourself in your creative endeavors is indeed what it is all about.

Tom Brierton
Chicago, Illinois

Glossary

additive technique—the process of adding material, such as clay or foam, onto a sculpture to create shapes.

arcs—the imaginary lines (straight or curved) that go through various points of the sculpture, giving the work its shape, contour, expression, and feel.

ball and socket armature—a skeletal understructure for a stop-motion puppet, machined from metal, in the shape of the puppet.

build-up technique—the process of building up foam (polyurethane and/or hot foam) over an existing armature.

casting—the actual sculpture that is removed from a mold (such as a foam casting of a puppet from a plaster or Ultracal mold).

color scheme—the color or colors that an artist chooses for a piece of art.

convection oven—a special type of oven that circulates and maintains heat throughout its chamber, providing even and consistent heat during the baking of the hot foam latex.

da Vinci pose—a pose that refers to Leonardo da Vinci's drawing, "Vitrovian Man." It depicts a standing man with double sets of arms and legs. The arms are held perpendicular and by his side, and the legs are held straight, as well as spread.

dry mount—the process of applying rubber cement to two different surfaces. Both surfaces are allowed to dry, then the parts are pressed together. A very strong bond is subsequently created.

epoxy putty—usually a two-part putty substance, with one part being a hardener, and the other part being a resin. Equal measures of the two parts are blended together until the mixture has a uniform color; after a period of time, the combination solidifies into an extremely hard mass.

exoskeleton—the outer supportive shell of an invertebrate, like an insect or crab.

flashing—the webbing that occurs on a foam casting while it is inside the mold.

foam core—a sturdy flat piece of matte-like board that can be easily cut and shaped.

foam injection technique—the process of mixing and injecting hot foam into a plaster or Ultracal mold.

foam skins—hot foam, which is mixed, then poured onto a flat smooth surface. Once it solidifies, the foam can be peeled from the surface and used for the skins of a built-up or foam injected puppet.

hemp—a plant fiber used to make cloth. When dipped in plaster or Ultracal and allowed to dry, the fibrous cloth creates a very strong mold.

injection gun—a device used in foam injection. Mixed hot foam is poured into the gun, and a plunger forces the foam into the mold cavity.

key pose—in animation jargon, the pose of a drawing, computer character, or puppet that holds the thought and essence of what the animated character is feeling, thinking, and doing.

kinetic sculpture—freestanding or hanging

sculpture that moves in real-time, either through natural phenomenon (such as wind or water), or by mechanical or electronic means.

lazy Susan—two flat pieces of metal that are connected by ball bearings. One piece can rotate independent of the other.

mold—a chamber (usually in two or more sections) made from plaster, ultracal, metal, etc., into which is injected or poured a liquid substance. Once dried or cooled, the liquid solidifies and is then extracted from the mold.

mold cavity—the interior of a mold, which forms the casting.

morgue file—a collection of drawings, photos, images, etc. of miscellaneous flora, fauna, animals, or anything else. These images are used by an artist for reference during the creation of art.

oven buckle belts—belts that tie together the pieces of a mold so that the mold does not come apart during the casting process.

physiology—the study of how an organic body functions via muscles, skin, internal organs, etc.

plaster—a powdery gypsum which, when mixed with water, will in time solidify to a hard substance suitable for making molds or sculptures.

polyurethane foam—a soft or rigid polymer foam that can be cut with scissors or a knife.

potter's wheel—a rotating table that spins a piece of water-soluble clay, which is in turn formed by the hands of a potter.

prototype—a fundamental design (usually in three dimensions) that acts as the primary design of a particular object.

prying keys—the small openings around the outer perimeter of a mold that allow for one to insert a pry bar for separating the mold halves.

"Puppetoon"—a puppet-animated short during the 1930s and '40s developed by filmmaker George Pal, which relied on the use of replacement figures.

pylon dowel rod—a rod support for a sculpture.

real-time—events that occur in the moment.

registration keys—pieces of clay, which are introduced around the outer perimeter of a mold.

Once the mold is created and allowed to dry, these clay key inserts are removed, thus revealing small holes into which a pry bar is inserted for the separation of the mold halves.

release agent—a substance that can be rubbed onto the surface of a mold half, so that when a liquid material is poured or injected into the mold, it (the casting) may be easily removed.

re-position—The proper placement and alignment of a machined or wire armature inside the center of a mold prior to the closing of the mold.

resin—a thermo-liquid substance (usually in two parts: a resin and a hardener) which, when mixed in equal parts, solidifies chemically.

running—the actual process of mixing and injecting hot foam into a mold.

slush casting—the act of taking mixed hot foam and pouring it into a mold or mold half. The mold is then rocked back and forth to allow the foam to seep into the mold impressions to create the casting.

stop-motion—the process of starting and stopping a motion picture or video camera to create either a pixilation or an animated character(s).

subtractive technique—the process of taking away (subtracting) from a hard substance (such as wood, plaster, stone, or marble) to create a sculpture.

taxidermist—one who engages in the art and science of preserving dead animals, especially vertebrates, usually for museum displays.

tie-down—a screw that comes up from beneath a table with many holes, and is then screwed into a threaded hole of an animated puppet's foot.

Ultracal 30—a powdery substance which, when mixed with water, can be used to create a mold. It sets at room temperature into a very hard matter.

Universal Colorant—the brand name for a kind of paint that is used for animation puppets.

Van Aiken clay—a brand of plasticene clay (clay that can be sculpted, or melted and poured) that comes in a variety of colors and is used for sculpting stop-motion puppets.

References

Supplies

Barge Cement

Quabaug Corporation
18 School Street
North Brookfield , MA 01535
www.vibram.com
508-867-7731

GM Foam

http://www.gmfoam.com
1-800-521-9520

Gram Scale

Scales Galore
431 Avenue U
Brooklyn, NY 11223
Phone: (718) 336-5900
http://www.scalesgalore.com

Minipocketscale.com
612 High Meadows Drive
Weatherford, TX 76088
817-594-5079
http://www.minipocketscale.com/balance_beam/3_
    beam_balance.htm

Polyurethane Foam

Hancock Fabrics
6310 W Touhy Ave
Niles, IL 60714

Hancock Fabrics
4030 Chino Hills Parkway
Chino Hills, CA
909-393-9663

Royal Touch
1037 Venice Blvd.
Los Angeles, CA
310-475-4755

Prosthetic Adhesive

Grand Stage Company, Inc.
630 W. Lake Street
Chicago, IL 60615
312-332-5611

Sunbeam Mixer

Goodman's
13130 SW 128 Street #3
Miami, FL 33186
1-888-333-4660

Ultracal 30

http://www.getspfx.com
(This product can also be purchased at most art
    stores houses that carry sculpting supplies.)

Universal Colorant

Pearl Art & Craft Supply, Inc.
225 West Chicago Avenue
Chicago IL 60610
312/915-0200

Sculpting Reference Books

Anatomy for the Artist.
Jeno Barcsay.
Barnes and Noble, by arrangement with Little, Brown and Co., Ltd. (UK), 1993. (First Hungarian edition 1953.)

Rodin — Sculptures and Drawings.
Catherine Lampert.
The Arts Council of Great Britain, 1986.
ISBN: 0-300-03807.

Essential Michelangelo.
Kirsten Bradbury.
Parragon, 2000.
ISBN: 0-75255-147-7.

Gray's Anatomy.
Henry Gray.
Running Press, 1974.
ISBN: 0-89471-135-0.

Index